First Survival of
Alzheimer's

First Survival of ALZHEIMER'S

Healed by **Holy Spirit**

ELMO HUDSON

First Survival of Alzheimer's

Copyright © 2019 by Elmo Hudson. All rights reserved.

No part of this publication may be reproduced, stored in a retrieval system or transmitted in any way by any means, electronic, mechanical, photocopy, recording or otherwise without the prior permission of the author except as provided by USA copyright law.

The opinions expressed by the author are not necessarily those of URLink Print and Media.

1603 Capitol Ave., Suite 310 Cheyenne, Wyoming USA 82001
1-888-980-6523 | admin@urlinkpublishing.com

URLink Print and Media is committed to excellence in the publishing industry.

Book design copyright © 2019 by URLink Print and Media. All rights reserved.

Published in the United States of America
ISBN 978-1-64367-845-0 (Paperback)
ISBN 978-1-64367-844-3 (Digital)

Non-Fiction
16.09.19

CONTENTS

Deligated Authority..82

Thoughts 85

Alzheimer's Bedridden - Healings and Miracles 90

Alzhemer's Appointment 96

My Christian life from September 5, 1972 when I was baptized with the Holy Spirit with the evidence of speaking in a heavenly language. I am going to explain how dedicated I was as a young babe in Christ. I went on a ten day fast after I received the baptism of the Holy Spirit on a Tuesday night. I made it seven days without water and ten days without food. Then I went on a fast for five days without food or water. And I tried to do it for four days, then for three days a week. And it was really hard on me, so I started fasting two days in each week for six years straight. I accomplished all this when I was a young single brother in Christ. After about three and a half years I started praying for a wife and the Lord answered my prayer but He did not give me what I asked for but what I needed so I could grow prosper, mature and develop in the things of the Lord. (My oldest sister Jesterine Quinn had a dream that a sister in Christ that she had witness to when they both were in the tenth grade at Sexton High School was going to become my wife. And her name was Cathie Cobb. And the same Christian had a dream that I was going to become a born-again Christian in the Pentecostal Faith.

And my Pastor brother Claude Young who was white had the same identical dream. At first, he told her that he had a dream that Cathie and Elmo were getting married and when he told me he said he had a dream that Cathie and I was getting married and he had told her and she said did you tell Elmo? My oldest sister also had a dream that I was going to be filled with the Holy Spirit, and my Mother Elizabeth Pearl 'Mitchell' Hudson said she knew it before my sister had her dream). The revival that I received the baptism of the Holy Spirit started on September 4, 1972 Through September 15, 1972 at Reverend Perry Robinson Church of God in Christ and

Reverend Jesse Lee Williams was in charge. Now back to my fasting life. I fasted two more days in September 1972. I fasted the next week for two days which was from Sunday night till Tuesday night. I think it was until ten thirty. Then my fast was over. I was so much in the Spirit, so I started another fast from Wednesday afternoon about two thirty in the afternoon until Saturday at two thirty in the afternoon. This was a three day fast (PRAISE GOD). Praise His Wonderful Holy name. Is not God wonderful? Amen!

I fasted one day on the sixth or seventh of October. I fasted on the eighth to the ninth of October. I fasted from the ninth to the tenth of October. I fasted again, for three days for my Father 'Jesus Christ'. I said Father as a new born babe in Christ. Now I know God is the Father and Jesus Christ is His son. I fasted again from twelve of October to the fourteen of October. I fasted two more days without bread or water. I fasted for five more days for the success of the soul witness of our Savior Jesus Christ and for giving me this new job. I fasted three more days without bread or water. I fasted three days without bread or water. I fasted for one day without bread or water. I will fast again for two days. I fasted three more days without bread or water (Praise God). I fasted two more days without water or food. I fasted three more days without bread or water. I fasted two days without bread or water. I fasted two more days to end the year of December 31, 1972. I also went to a Church service four times that day and went to a musical in Jackson Michigan till about 3:10 A.M. 'WOW'. I am endeavoring to go all the way to perfection this year (Praise God).

I am now in the process of starting my Spiritual life of fasting for '1973'. I fasted one day and the devil tried to put the flu on me, but I did not claim it. I fasted two days this time without food or water. I am going to give God two days each week. I fasted one hundred and four days this year (Praise God). Praise His wonderful Holy name. I wanted to give God three days this week, because I wanted to be up to date with giving God two days a week, but Praise God He gave me another day, so I was blessed to give God four days this week (Praise God). All I have to do is take a step-in faith and let faith have its perfect work in my life (Praise God). I started another fast, but I stopped with only three hours to go before I would have had one full day, but someone at work brought me a piece of cake, so I ate it foolishly and I felt so bad. Then the scripture came to me in I SAMUEL 15:22 And Samuel said, "Hath the Lord as great delight in burnt offerings and sacrifices, as in obeying the voice of the Lord? Behold, to obey is better than sacrifice, and to hearken than the fat of rams. (23) For rebellion is as the sin of witchcraft, and stubbornness is as iniquity and idolatry. Because thou hast rejected the word of the Lord (24) And Saul said unto Samuel, I have sinned: For I have transgressed the commandment of the Lord, and thy words: because I feared the people, and obeyed their voice. (25) Now therefore, I pray thee, pardon my sin, and turn again with me, that I may worship the Lord (26) And Samuel said unto Saul, I will not return with thee: For thou hast rejected the word of the Lord, and the Lord hath rejected thee from being king over Israel. (I was just a new Christian in Christ and that had been instilled in my heart to be like Christ). Therefore, I started my fast all over again for two whole days. Afterwards I completed another two days of fasting (Praise God).

The next week I fasted for three days this week and I really felt the present of the Lord (Praise God). The next week I fasted for two days without food or water (Praise God). The next week I fasted for three days without food or water (Praise God). Praise His wonderful Holy name. The next week I fasted for two days without food or water (Praise God). I fasted the next week for two days without food or water (Praise God). I fasted two more days without food or water (Praise God). I fasted two more days the next week without bread or water (Praise God). I fasted three days the next week without bread or water (Praise God). The Church went to the General Gathering in Eldorado, Illinois on May 5, 1973 (Praise God).

I am mounting up higher and higher in Christ Jesus. I fasted two more days, without bread and water ending week of May 20, 1973 (Praise God). I fasted two more days, without bread or water ending on week of May 25, 1973 (Praise God). I fasted two more days ending week of June 8, 1973 (Praise God). I believe God has giving me a new revelation on fasting, instead of fasting two days in a row, to just fast two days in every week; for instance, to eat one day then fast a day. Then eat the next day and fast the next day to give me a total of two days each week (Praise God). This will make things easier and give me more strength to study the bible and listen to my cassette tapes and read my notes that I write down doing bible study on Saturdays and teaching and worshiping services on Sundays in Sunday school and teaching and testifying services. I have learned that God through His Son Jesus looks out for my best interest, because I am obedient to the faith (Praise God).

I fasted two more days without bread and water ending week of June 15, 1973 (Praise God). I fasted two more days without bread and water ending week of July 13, 1973 (Praise God). I fasted two more days without bread or water the last part of July 1973 (Praise God). I fasted two more days without bread and water in the first week of August 3, 1973 (Praise God). I made an exception and fasted two days in a row ending on August 11, 1973 (Praise God). I fasted two more days ending on August 18, 1973 (Praise God). I fasted two more days without bread and water ending on August 24, 1973 (Praise God). The last week I fasted two days without bread and water ending Friday on August 31, 1973 (Praise God). I fasted two more days without bread and water ending the first week of September 7, 1973 (Praise God). I fasted two more days without bread and water in the week of September 15, 1973 (Praise God). I fasted two more days without bread and water ending week of September 22, 1973 while on vacation totaling six days all together, twice each week (Praise God).

I fasted two days this week without bread and water after coming back from vacation from October 15 through October 21, 1973 (Praise God). I fasted two more days without bread and water ending week of October 28, 1973 (Praise God). I fasted two more days without bread and water ending on November 1, 1973 (Praise God). I fasted two more days without bread and water ending week of November 12, 1973 (Praise God). I fasted two more days without bread and water ending on November 18, 1973 (Praise God). I fasted two more days without bread and water in the week ending on November 25, 1973 (Praise God). I fasted two more days without bread and water ending the last week of November 30, 1973 (Praise

God). I fasted two more days without bread and water in the week of December 8, 1973 (Praise God). I fasted two more days without bread and water ending on December 14, 1973 (Praise God). I fasted two more days without bread and water ending week of December 23, 1973 (Praise God). I fasted two more days without bread and water ending the last week of December 31, 1973 (Praise God). I total one hundred and four days ending the year of December 31, 1973 (Praise God). The last two days I was visiting in San Pablo, California in the bay area of Berkley, Oakland, and San Francisco for Christmas Holidays and going to revivals with my brother-in-law Evangelist John C. Quinn and his wife Jesterine 'Hudson' Quinn who had a nice singing voice (Praise God).

I am starting my Spiritual life for 1974. I am going too fast for a total of one hundred and four days each year. I fasted two days in the first week of January of 1974 (Praise God). I fasted two more days in the second week of 1974 (Praise God). I fasted two more days in the week of January 20, 1974 (Praise God). I fasted two more days in the week of January 27, 1974 (Praise God). I fasted two more days ending week of February 3, 1974 (Praise God). I fasted two more days ending in the week of February 10, 1974 (Praise God). I fasted two more days ending week of February 17, 1974 (Praise God). I fasted for two days and then I fasted another day for a total of three days ending in the last week of February 28, 1974 (Praise God).

I fasted two more days in the week of March 8, 1974 (Praise God). I fasted two more days ending week of March 15, 1974 (Praise God). I fasted three days the next week but I gave myself credit for two days because of being disobedient to the Lord of heaven, ending week of March 24, 1974 (Praise God). In the month of April, I-7, 1974 I fasted for two days (Praise God). I fasted two more days in the week of April 11, 1974 (Praise God). I fasted two more days in the week of April 20. 1974 (Praise God). I fasted three days in the week of May 3, 1974 (Praise God). I fasted two more days in the week ending May 9, 1974 (Praise God). I fasted two more days ending the week of May 19, 1974 (Praise God). I fasted two more days in the week of May 26, 1974 (Praise God). I fasted two more days ending the month of May 31, 1974 (Praise God).

I fasted two more days in the first week of June 7, 1974 (Praise God). I fasted two more days ending the second week of June 14, 1974 (Praise God). I fasted two more days in the week of June 23, 1974 (Praise God). I fasted two more days ending week of June 30, 1974 at a Church of God in Christ Youth Conference Convention in Kansas City Missouri, when I was praying and seeking for a wife since there were no young ladies at our local Gospel Assembly Church and no 'BLACKS' around my age at any of our Churches which was mostly from the Southern States. I fasted two more days in the week of July 14, 1974 (Praise God). This week I went on a three day fast ending week of July 21, 1974 (Praise God).

I would rather be ahead in my fasting to God than be behind and having to make up those days of fasting (Praise God). I fasted three more days in the first week of August 1, 1974 (Praise God). I always fast without bread or water or anything else. I go through it with the Holy Spirit of God and His grace is sufficient. I fasted two more days ending on August 10, 1974 (Praise God). I fasted two more days, then I ate too much, so I had to make the days up to the Lord Jesus, so I started my fast over again in the same week, ending on August 17, 1974 (Praise God).

I fasted two more days ending in the week of August 25, 1974 (Praise God). I fasted two more days and I did not feel comfortable or the way I thought I should feel, so I started the two day fast over again and I received a great blessing because I received a revelation from Jesus, The Son of the Living God in the week of August 31, 1974 (Praise God). I fasted two more days, and one of those days I did not feel comfortable with; so, I fasted two more days to make up for that one day ending on September 15, 1974 (Praise God). Then I started another two day fast ending the week of September 22, 1974 (Praise God). I fasted two more days ending week of September 30, 1974 (Praise God). I fasted three days in the weekend of October 6, 1974 (Praise God). I fasted two more days in the week of October 13, 1974 (Praise God). I went on another two day fast in the week of October 20, 1974 (Praise God). I fasted two more days in the week of October 27, 1974 (Praise God). I fasted two more days in the week of November 3, 1974 (Praise God).

I fasted two more days in the week of November 10, 1974 (Praise God). I fasted two more days without eating food or drinking any water or anything, just before I went to our youth conference in Saint Louis, Missouri, ending the week of November 27, 1974 (Praise God). I fasted two whole days without food or water after the youth conference which started on November 29, 1974, through December 1, 1974 (Praise God). And my fast ended on December 5, 1974 (Praise God). I went on a three day fast in the week of December 22, 1974, to end the year striving to overcome sin, so I can come on the same level and plateau as Jesus who 1 Peter 2:21-25 said that he was our example (Praise God).

I fasted two more days on December 23 to December 25, 1974 (Praise God). I wrote down I am going too fast for two days each week for a total of one hundred and four days in the year of 1975 (Praise God). I fasted three days in the first week of January 1, 1975. I started at 12 P.M. till 12:02 P.M on January 3, 1975 (Praise God). I had a few trials on the first few hours of my fast, but Jesus Christ strengthen me and I got through it with great inspiration from the Holy Spirit (Praise God). I fasted for two days straight without bread or water and ended the week of January 12, 1975 (Praise God). I fasted two more days in the week of January 26, 1975 (Praise God). I fasted two more days in the week of February 2, 1975 (Praise God). I fasted two more days trying to keep my mind on Jesus and Holiness but my mind went to seed on a thought and I had to regroup my thoughts by keeping my mind on one accord just like I had been taught to keep my mind girded up on Spiritual things (Praise God). This ended the week of February 16, 1975 (Praise God). I fasted two more days without bread or water in the week of February 23, 1975 (Praise God). I fasted two more days without food or water ending the week of March 2, 1975 (Praise God).

I fasted two more days without food or water in the week of March 9, 1975 (Praise God). I fasted two more days without food or water in the week of March 16, 1975 (Praise God). I fasted two more days without food or water in the week of March 23, 1975 (Praise God). I fasted two more days without bread or water in the week of March 30, 1975 (Praise God). I am now starting my fast for the Month of April 1975) I fasted two days without food or water in the week of April 6, 1975 (Praise God). I fasted two more days without bread or water in the week of April 13, 1975 (Praise God). I fasted two more days without bread and water, I notice I said fasting without bread or water; instead of without bread and water, which means I always went on a total fast without food and water; not anything at all. Jesus the only begotten Son of Jehovah God suffered and was crucified for our sins and I am His disciple or follower and he has set the example of whom we are to pattern our lives after, then it's a pleasure to suffer for the cause of Christ.

I fasted two more days without bread and water in the week of April 20, 1975 (Praise God). I am now starting my fast for the Month of May of 1975 (Praise God). I fasted two days in the week of May 11, 1975 (Praise God). I became sick after coming back from our General Gathering when all of our Churches come together for a great fellowship meeting two to three times a year for three days in St Louis Missouri. I never quit or give in to the flesh I continued to live and work naturally and spiritually. I fasted for two more days without bread and water in the week of May 18, 1975 (Praise God). I fasted two more days without bread and water in the week of May 25, 1975 (Praise God).

I am now going to start my Fast for the month of June, 1975 (Praise God). I fasted two days without food or water in the week of June 8, 1975 (Praise God). I fasted two more days without bread and water in the week of June 15, 1975 (Praise God). I fasted two more days without food and water in the week of June 22, 1975 (Praise God). I fasted two more days without bread and water in the week of June 29, 1975 (Praise God). I am now starting my fast for the month of July of 1975. I fasted two days in the week of July 6, 1975 (Praise God). I fasted two more days without bread and water in the week of July 13, 1975 (Praise God). I fasted two more days without bread and water in the week of July 20, 1975 (Praise God). I started my fast for the month of August of 1975 (Praise God). I fasted two straight days without bread or water or resting in between those two days ending the week of August 10, 1975 (Praise God). I went on another fast for two straight days without any rest between those two days and without bread and water in the week of August 17, 1975 (Praise God). I fasted two more days without bread and water in the week of August 24, 1975 (Praise God). I fasted two more days without bread and water ending the month of August 31, 1975 (Praise God).

I am starting my fast for the month of September of 1975 (Praise God). I fasted two more days without bread and water in the week of September 7, 1975, And on to perfection to an overcoming life (Praise God). I fasted two more days without bread and water in the week of September 14, 1975 (Praise God). This is what I wrote after this fast? I am going to overcome this fleshly mind, so I can stay in the Spirit, starting on September 13, 1975 (Praise God). And on to perfection or an overcoming life, so I can be just like Jesus. I fasted two more days without bread and water ending week of September 21, 1975 (Praise God). I fasted two more days without bread and water ending week of September 28, 1975 (Praise God).

I started my fast for the month of October of 1975. I fasted two days without bread and water for two whole days ending the week of October 5, 1975 (Praise God). I fasted two more days without bread and water ending week of October 12, 1975 (Praise God). I fasted two more days without food and water ending week of October 19, 1975 (Praise God). I fasted two more days without bread and water ending the week of October 26, 1975 (Praise God). I am starting my fast for the month of November of 1975 (Praise God). I fasted two days without bread and water in the week of November 2, 1975 (Praise God). I fasted two more days without food and water ending week of November 9, 1975 (Praise God). I fasted two more days without bread and water in the week of November16, 1975 (Praise God). I fasted two more days without food or water in the week of November 23, 1975 (Praise God). I fasted two more days without bread and water ending week of November 30, 1975, without ceasing (Praise God).

I started my fast for the month of December of 1975. I fasted two more days without bread and water ending week of December 8, 1975 (Praise God). I fasted two more days without bread and water ending week of December 21, 1975 (Praise God). I fasted two more days without bread and water ending week of December 28, 1975

(Praise God). I have ended the year of 1975 with praises unto the king Jesus Christ by fasting to show my love for Christ the Son of the living God (Praise God).

I am going to start my fast for the year of 1976 (Praise God). I am doing this for the purpose of showing my love and appreciation to the King Jesus whom all blessings flow. In the first week I fasted two days without bread and water ending week of January 4, 1976 (Praise God). I fasted two more days without bread and water ending week of January the second and third of 1976 (Praise God). I ended my fast after five O'clock (Praise God). I fasted two more days without bread and water in the week of January 11, 1976 (Praise God). I fasted two more days without bread and water ending week of January 17, 1976 (Praise God). I fasted two more days without bread and water ending week of January 25, 1976 (Praise God). I fasted two more days without bread and water ending week of February 1, 1976 (Praise God). I have fasted two more days straight without bread and water ending in the week February 7, 1976 (Praise God). I fasted two more days without bread and water ending week of February 14, 1976 (Praise God). I fasted two straight days without bread and water ending week of February 22, 1976 (Praise God). I fasted two more days without bread or water, ending week of February 29, (Praise God).

I am starting my fast for the month of March of 1976 (Praise God). I fasted two days without bread and water ending week of March 7, 1976 (Praise God). I fasted two more days without bread and water ending week of March 14, 1976 (Praise God). I fasted two more days without bread and water ending week of March 21, 1976 (Praise God). I fasted two more days without eating or drinking anything in the week of March 28, 1976 (Praise God).

I am starting my fast for the Month of April of 1976 (Praise God). I fasted two more days without eating or drinking anything ending week of April 4, 1976 (Praise God). I fasted two more days without eating or water ending week of April 11, 1976 (Praise God). 'Palm Sunday' I fasted two more days without food or drink ending week of April 18, 1976 (Praise God). I fasted two more days without food or drink ending week of April 25, 1976 (Praise God).

I am starting my fast for the month of May of 1976 (Praise God). I fasted two days without food or drink in the week of May 2, 1976 (Praise God). I fasted two more days without bread or water ending week of May 9, 1976 (Praise God). I fasted two more days without bread or water in the week of May 16, 1976 (Praise God). I fasted two more days without bread and water ending week of May 23, 1976 (Praise God). I fasted two more days without eating or drinking anything ending the last week of May 30, 1976 (Praise God). I am starting my fast for the month of June of 1976 (Praise God). I fasted two days without eating or drinking anything in the week of June 6, 1976 (Praise God). I fasted two more days without bread and water in the week of June 13, 1976 (Praise God). I fasted two more days without food or drink ending week of June 20, 1976 (Praise God). I fasted two more days straight through without food or drink in the week of June 27, 1976 (Praise God).

I started my fast for the month of July of 1976 (Praise God). I fasted two days without food or drink in the week ending July 4, 1976 (Praise God). 'Declaration of Independence Day' I fasted two more days without food or drink ending week of July 11, 1976 (Praise God). I fasted two more days without food and drink ending week of July 18, 1976 (Praise God). I fasted two more days without bread or water ending week of July 25, 1976 (Praise God). I started my fast for the month of August of 1976 (Praise God). I fasted two days straight without bread or water in the month of August 1, 1976 (Praise God). I fasted two more days without bread or water in the week of August 8, 1976 (Praise God). I fasted two more days without bread or water ending week of August 15, 1976 (Praise God). I was on a fast for two days and I mistakenly took a drink of water when I was going to Lansing Community College on my U.S Army G.I. Bill majoring in Religion or Philosophy to learn the historical part of the bible, and I graduated with an Associate Degree in '1981' I started the complete fast all over again, going two full days without bread or water (Praise God).

I fasted two more days without bread and water ending week of August 22, 1976 (Praise God). I fasted two more days ending week of August 29, 1976 (Praise God). I started my fast for the month of

September 5, 1976 (Praise God). I fasted two days ending week of September 5, 1976 (Praise God). I fasted two more days ending week of September 12, 1976 (Praise God). I fasted three days this week without bread and water ending week of September 19, 1976 (Praise God). I fasted two more days without bread or water ending week of September 19, 1976 (Praise God). I fasted two more days without food or drink ending week of September 26, 1976 (Praise God).

I started my fast for the month of October 1976 (Praise God). I fasted two more days without bread or water in the week of October 10, 1976 (Praise God). I fasted two more days without bread and water ending week of October 17, 1976 (Praise God). I fasted two more days without bread or water ending week of October 31, 1976 (Praise God). I started my fast for the month of November 1976 (Praise God). I fasted two days ending week of November 7, 1976 (Praise God). I fasted two days without bread and water ending the week of November 14, 1976 (Praise God). I fasted two more days without bread or water in the week of November 21, 1976 (Praise God). I fasted two more days without food and drink ending the week of November 28, 1976 (Praise God).

I started my fast for the month of December 1976 (Praise God). I fasted for two days without bread or water during the week of December 5, 1976 (Praise God). I fasted two more days without bread and water ending week of December 12, 1976 (Praise God). I fasted two more days without bread or water during the week of December 19, 1976 (Praise God). I fasted for two more days without food or water during the week of December 26, 1976 (Praise God). I fasted two more days without bread or water ending the month of December 31, 1976 (Praise God). I started my Spiritual fast for the month of January 1977 (Praise God). I fasted two more days without bread and water ending week of January 9, 1977 (Praise God). I fasted two days without bread and water ending the week of January 16, 1977 (Praise God). I fasted two more days without food or drink during the week of January 16, 1977 (Praise God). I fasted two more days without bread and water during the week of January 23, 1977 (Praise God). I fasted two more days without bread and water during the week of January 30, 1977 (Praise God).

I am starting my fast for the month of February 1977 (Praise God). I fasted two days without bread or water for the week of February 6, 1977 (Praise God). I fasted two more days without bread or water for the week of February 13, 1977 (Praise God). I fasted two more days without food or drink during the week of February 20, 1977 (Praise God). I fasted two more days without food or drink for the week of February 27, 1977 (Praise God). I started my fast for the month of March 1977 (Praise God). I fasted two days without bread or water for the week of March 6, 1977 (Praise God). I fasted two more days without bread and water for the week of March 13, 1977 (Praise God). I fasted for two more days without bread or drink for the week of March 20, 1977 (Praise God). I fasted two more days without food or drink for the week of March 27, 1977 (Praise God).

I started my fast for the month of April 1977 (Praise God). I fasted two days without bread or water in the first week of April 3, 1977 (Praise God). I fasted two more days without bread or water ending the week of April 10, 1977 (Praise God). I fasted two more days without bread and water in the week of April 17, 1977 (Praise God). I fasted two more days without food or drink ending the week of April 24, 1977 (Praise God). I continued my fast through the month of May, 1977 (Praise God). I fasted for two days without bread and water ending on week of May 1, 1977 (Praise God). I fasted two more days without bread or water ending week of May 8, 1977 (Praise God). I fasted two more days without bread or water ending week of May 15, 1977 (Praise God). I fasted two more days without bread or water ending week of May 29, 1977 (Praise God).

I started my fast for the month of June 1977 (Praise God). I fasted two more days without bread and water ending week of June 5, 1977 (Praise God). I fasted two more days without bread and water for two straight days ending week of June 12, 1977 (Praise God). I fasted one day without bread and water; then I went on a two day fast without bread or water for two days straight without skipping a day ending week of June 19, 1977 (Praise God). This was also in the same week that my brother-in-law Evangelist John C. Quinn was running a revival in Lansing, Michigan (Praise God). I fasted two days straight without skipping a day without bread and water in the week ending June 27, 1977 (Praise God). I started my fast for the month of July of 1977 (Praise God). I fasted two days without food or drink in the week of July 3, 1977 (Praise God). I fasted two more days without bread or water in the week of July 10, 1977 (Praise God). I fasted two more days without bread and water in the week of July 17, 1977 (Praise God). I fasted two more days without food or drink in the week of July 25, 1977 (Praise God). I fasted two more days without food or drink ending week of July 31, 1977 (Praise God). I am beginning my fast for the month of August 1977 (Praise God). I fasted two days without bread of water in the week of August 7, 1977 (Praise God). I fasted two more days without food or drink in the week of August 14, 1977 (Praise God). I fasted two more days without bread or water ending week of August 20, 1977 (Praise God) I fasted two more days without bread and water ending week of August 28, 1977 (Praise God).

I am starting my fast for the month of September 1977 (Praise God). I fasted for two days without food or drink in the week of September 4, 1977 (Praise God). I fasted two more days without bread and water in the week of September 11, 1977 (Praise God). I fasted two more days without food or drink in the week of September 18, 1977 (Praise God). I fasted two more days without bread or water in the week of September 25, 1977 (Praise God).

I started my fast for the month of October of 1977 (Praise God). I fasted for two days without food or drink in the week of October 2, 1977 (Praise God). I fasted two days without food or drink in the week of October 9, 1977 (Praise God). I fasted two more days without bread and water ending week of October 16, 1977 (Praise God). I fasted two more days without bread or water in the week of October 23, 1977 (Praise God). I fasted two more days without bread and water ending week of October 30, 1977 (Praise God).

I started my fast for the month of November 1977 (Praise God). I fasted two days without food or drink in the week of November 6, 1977 (Praise God). I fasted two days without food or drink in the week of November 13, 1977 (Praise God). I fasted two more days without food or drink in the week of November 20, 1977 (Praise

God). I fasted two more days without bread or water ending week of November 27, 1977 (Praise God).

I am beginning my fast for the month of December 1977 (Praise God). I fasted two days without bread and water in the week of December 4, 1977 (Praise God). I fasted two more days without bread and water ending week of December 11, 1977 (Praise God). I fasted two more days without bread and water in the week of December 25, 1977 (Praise God). I fasted two more days without bread and water ending the week of December 31, 1977, closing out the year of 1977 (Praise God).

I am in the process of starting my Holy Spirit fast for the year of January 1978 (Praise God). I fasted three days straight without bread or water in the month ending June 2, 1978 (Praise God). I fasted two more days without bread and water ending week of January 15, 1978 (Praise God). I fasted two more days without bread and water ending week of January 22, 1978 (Praise God). I fasted two more days without bread and water ending week of January 29, 1978 (Praise God).

I begin my fast for the month of February 1978 (Praise God). I fasted two more days without bread and water in the week of February 5, 1978 (Praise God). I fasted two more days without food or drink in the week of February 12, 1978 (Praise God). I fasted two more days without bread and water in the week of February 19, 1978 (Praise God). I fasted two more days without bread and water ending week of February 26, 1978 (Praise God).

I am starting my fast for the month of March 1978 (Praise God). I fasted two days without bread and water in the first week of March 5, 1978 (Praise God). I fasted two more days in the week of March 12, 1978 (Praise God). I fasted two more days without food and drink in the week of March 19, 1978 (Praise God). I fasted three days this week without bread and water ending week of March 26, 1978 (Praise God).

I am starting my fast for the month of April 1978 (Praise God). I fasted two days without food or water in the week of April 2, 1978 (Praise God). I fasted two more days without bread or water in the week of April 9, 1978 (Praise God). I fasted two more days in the week of April 16, 1978 (Praise God). I fasted two more days without food or drink ending week of April 23, 1978 (Praise God). I fasted two more days without bread or water ending week of April 30, 1978 (Praise God).

I am starting my fast for the month of May 1978 (Praise God). I fasted two days without bread and water in the week of May 7, 1978 (Praise God). I fasted two more days ending week of May 14, 1978 (Praise God). I fasted two more days without food or drink in the week of May 21, 1978 (Praise God). I fasted two more days without food or drink ending the week of May 28, 1978 (Praise God).

I am beginning my fast for the month of June 1978 (Praise God). I fasted two days without bread and water in the first week of June 4, 1978 (Praise God). I fasted two more days without bread and water in the week of June 11, 1978 (Praise God). I fasted two more days without bread and water in the week of June 18, 1978 (Praise God). I fasted two more days without bread and water in the week of June 25, 1978 (Praise God). I fasted three days this week without bread and water going into the month of July 2, 1978 (Praise God). I fasted two more days without bread and water in the week of July 9, 1978 (Praise God). I fasted two more days without food or drink in the week of July 16, 1978 (Praise God). I fasted this week with my new bride of July 15, 1978 and together we went on a three day fast without missing a day without bread and water ending the week of July 30, 1978 (Praise God).

I started my fast for the month of August 1978 (Praise God). I fasted two days without food or drink in the week of August 6, 1978 (Praise God). I fasted two days straight without skipping a day without bread or water in the week of August 13, 1978 (Praise God). I fasted two more days without bread or juice in the week of August 20, 1978 (Praise God). I fasted two more days without food or water in the week of August 27, 1978 (Praise God). I fasted two days without bread and water in the week September 3, 1978 (Praise God). I fasted two more days without food or juice in the week of September 10, 1978 (Praise God). I fasted two more days without bread or water in the week of September17, 1978 (Praise

FIRST SURVIVAL OF ALZHEIMER'S

God). I fasted two more days without bread or juice in the week of September 24, 1978 (Praise God).

I started my fast for the month of October 1978 (Praise God). I fasted two days without bread and water for the week of October 8, 1978 (Praise God). I fasted two more days without bread or water for the week of October 15, 1978 (Praise God). I fasted two more days without bread and water for the week of October 22, 1978 (Praise God). I fasted four days every other day without bread and water for the week of October 29, 1978 (Praise God).

I started my fast for the month of November 1978 (Praise God). I fasted two days without food or drink for the week of November 5, 1978 (Praise God). I fasted for three days this week without bread and water in the week of November 12, 1978 (Praise God). I fasted three more days without bread or water in the week of November 19, 1978 (Praise God). I fasted two days without bread and water for the week of November 26, 1978 (Praise God).

I began my fast for the month of December 1978 (Praise God). I fasted two days without food or drink for the week of December 3, 1978 (Praise God). I fasted two more days without bread or juice in the week of December 10, 1978 (Praise God). I fasted two more days without bread and water for the week of December 17, 1978 (Praise God). My Holy Spirit Filled Life of December 1979 (Praise God). I fasted two days without bread and water for the week of January 7, 1979 (Praise God). I fasted two more days without bread or juice in the week of January 14, 1979 (Praise God). I fasted two more days without bread and water for the week of January 28, 1979 (Praise God).

I am beginning my fast for the month of February 1979 (Praise God). I fasted two days without bread and water for the week of February 4, 1979 (Praise God). I fasted two more days without bread and water for the week of February 11, 1979 (Praise God). I fasted two more days without food or juice in the week of February 18, 1979 (Praise God). I fasted two more days without bread and juice in the week of February 25, 1979 (Praise God). I started my fast for the month of March 1979 (Praise God). I fasted two days without bread and water in the week of March 4, 1979 (Praise God). I fasted two more days without bread and juice for the week of March 11, 1979 (Praise God). I fasted two more days without bread and juice in the week of March 18, 1979 (Praise God). I fasted two more days without bread and water for the week of March 25, 1979 (Praise God).

I started my fast for the month of April 1979 (Praise God). I fasted two days without bread and water in the week of April 8, 1979 (Praise God). I fasted two more days without bread and juice in the week of April 15, 1979 (Praise God). (EASTER SUNDAY) I was fasting and someone on my job at General Motors offered me a piece of cake and I accepted it without thinking, then it came to me I was on my fast. I started my fast for that day over again, and I only had fifteen minutes to go and my fast would have been over; but my conscience condemn me and as usual I started that day all over again (Praise God). 'I look back to those days and the love and dedication that I had for the Son of God'. I fasted two more days without bread or water in the week of April 22, 1979 (Praise God). I fasted two more days without bread and water for the week of April 29, 1979 (Praise God).

I started my fast for the month of May 1979 (Praise God). I fasted two days without bread and water in the week of May 6, 1979 (Praise God). I fasted two more days without bread and water in the week of May 13, 1979 (Praise God). I fasted three days this week without bread and water for the week of May 20, 1979 (Praise God). I fasted two more days without food or water for the week of May 27, 1979 (Praise God). I started my fast for the month of June 1979 (Praise God). I fasted two days without bread and water in the week of June 3, 1979 (Praise God). I fasted three more days without bread and water in the week of June 10, 1979 (Praise God). I fasted two more days without bread and juice in the week of June 17, 1979 (Praise God). I fasted two more days without bread and water in the week of June 24, 1979 (Praise God).

I started my fast for the month of July 1979 (Praise God). I fasted two days without bread and water in the week of July 1, 1979 (Praise God). I fasted two more days without bread and water for the week of July 8, 1979 (Praise God). I fasted two more days without bread and water for the week of July 15, 1979 (Praise God). I fasted two more days without bread and water for the week of July 22, 1979 (Praise God). I fasted two more days without food and juice for the week of July 29, 1979 (Praise God). I am starting my fast for the month of August 1979 (Praise God). I fasted two days straight without a break without bread and water for the week August 5, 1979 (Praise God). I fasted two more days straight without bread and water for the week of August 12, 1979 (Praise God). I fasted two more days straight without bread or juice in the week of August 19, 1979 (Praise God). I fasted two more days for the week of August 26, 1979 (Praise God). I fasted two more days without bread and water ending in the week of September 2, 1979 (Praise God).

I started my fast for the month of August 1979 (Praise God). I fasted for two days straight without missing a day without bread or water in the week of August 5, 1972 (Praise God). I fasted again for two more days straight without bread and water in the week of August 12, 1979 (Praise God). I fasted again for two straight days without bread or water for the week of August 19, 1979 (Praise God). I fasted two days without bread and water for the week of August 26, 1979 (Praise God). I started my fast for the month of September 1979 (Praise God). I fasted two days without bread and water for the week of September 2, 1979 (Praise God). I fasted two more days without bread and water in the week of September 9, 1979 (Praise God). I fasted two more days without bread and water in the week of September 16, 1979 (Praise God). I fasted two more days without food or water in the week of September 23, 1979 (Praise God). I fasted two more days without bread and juice for the week of September 30, 1979 (Praise God).

I begin my fast for the month of October 1979 (Praise God). I fasted two days without bread and water for the week of October 7, 1979 (Praise God). I fasted two more days without bread or juice for the week of October 14, 1979 (Praise God). I fasted two more days without bread and water for the week of October 21, 1979 (Praise God). I fasted two more days without bread and drink for the week of October 28, 1979 (Praise God). I started my fast for the month of November 1979 (Praise God). I fasted for two days without bread or juice for the week of November 4, 1979 (Praise God). I fasted two more days without bread or juice in the week of November 11, 1979 (Praise God). I fasted two more days without food or juice in the week of November 19, 1979 (Praise God). I fasted two more days without food or juice for the week of November 25, 1979 (Praise God). I started my fast for the month of December 1979 (Praise God). I fasted for two days without food or drink in the week of December 2, 1979 (Praise God). I fasted two more days without bread or water for the week of December 9, 1979 (Praise God). I fasted two more days without food or drink for the week of December 16, 1979 (Praise God). I fasted two more days without food or water for the week of December 23, 1979 (Praise God). I fasted two more days without bread or drink in the week of December 30, 1979 (Praise God). This closes out the year of December 31, 1979 (Praise God).

My Holy Spirit filled life of the beginning of the New Year of January of 1980 (Praise God). I fasted for two days without bread and water in the week of January 6, 1980 (Praise God). I fasted two more days without food or drink in the week of January 13, 1980 (Praise God). I fasted two more days without bread and water in the week of January 20, 1980 (Praise God). I fasted every other day for four days without bread and water in the week of January 27, 1980 (Praise God). I started my fast for the month of February 3, 1980 (Praise God). I fasted two more days without bread or drink in the week of February 10, 1980 (Praise God). I fasted two more days without bread and water for the week of February 17, 1980 (Praise God). I fasted two more days without bread and water for the week ending February 24, 1980 (Praise God).

I started my fast for the month of March of 1980 (Praise God). I fasted for two days without bread or water for the week of March 2, 1980 (Praise God). I fasted two days without bread and water for the week of March 9, 1980 (Praise God). I fasted for two more days without food or drink for the week of March 23, 1980 (Praise God). I fasted two more days without bread and water for the week of March 30, 1980 (Praise God). I started my fast for the month of April (Praise God). I fasted two days without bread and water in the week of April 6, 1980 (Praise God). I got sick in the week of April 20,

1980 but I continued fasting in the next week (Praise God). I fasted three days without bread or water for the week of April 27, 1980 (Praise God). I fasted two more days without bread and water for the week of April 30, 1980 (Praise God). I started my fast for the month of May of 1980 (Praise God). I fasted three days without bread and water in the week of May 4, 1980 (Praise God). I fasted two more days without bread and water for the week of May 11, 1980 (Praise God). I fasted two more days without bread and water in the week of May 18, 1980 (Praise God). I fasted two more days without food or drink in the week of May 25, 1980 (Praise God).

    I started my fast for the month of June 1980 (Praise God). I fasted for two days without bread and water that carried over from the month of May through the week of June 1, 1980 (Praise God). I fasted two more days without bread and water in the week of June 8, 1980 (Praise God). I fasted two more days without bread and water for the week of June 15, 1980 (Praise God). I fasted two more days without bread and water for the week of June 22, 1980 (Praise God). I fasted two more days without bread and drink for the week of June 29, 1980 (Praise God). I stated my fast for the month of July of 1980 (Praise God). I fasted for two days without bread and water in the week of July 6, 1980 (Praise God). I fasted two more days without bread and water for the week of July 13, 1980 (Praise God). I believe the Lord Jesus is talking to my heart concerning fasting that I don't need to fast two days each week; because it is not necessary anymore, since I have proven myself faithful in fasting twice each week, a total of one hundred and four days each year (Praise God). The bible said in Matthew 18: 16 if he will not hear thee, then take with thee one or two more, that in the mouth of two or three witnesses every word may be established.

    I got sick twice during change over working on the assembly line in the Kettering Engine Plant at General Motors Corporation main plant 1. I could only relief some of my people for their breaks since I was a relief man. I don't think I would have made it if the Lord had not Intervene in my behalf (Praise God). I cut my fast life in half through all indication God talked to my mind. I was sick for four days the first time before I went on a four day fast every other day. Then I got sick again then I felt led by the Spirit of God to end my eight years of fasting. I average about two days a week for almost eight years without bread and water ending in the week of August 17, 1980. I know without any further delay I had proven myself to God and His beloved Son Jesus Christ. During all this time I was the president of a witnessing group call The Deliverance Crusaders, where a group of us would meet every Saturday noon to go witnessing in pairs after having prayer and going over the materials preparing ourselves to go out into the projects to witness for Christ. I really enjoyed going out witnessing and many times I was on a fast and therefore, I was full of the Spirit of God and of Faith.

There is nothing like fasting and it gave me the power that I needed to abound in the things of the Lord. And before I would leave my house I would always prepare myself in studying the scriptures and memorizing them so I could answer those that would ask me a question about the work of the Lord. I believed I truly had a calling on my life to be a witness for Jesus Christ and win souls to the kingdom of God on earth. When I would pray before I would prepare myself to meet the witness group at a certain place we were to meet at. The Holy Spirit would come upon me and I would raise my hand and the Holy Spirit would begin to move my arms and hands just like when the wind is blowing and the branches and leaves move according to the swiftness of the wind. And I would began to speak in a heavenly language and the joy of the Holy Spirit would bring tears to my eyes and the most heavenly feeling in the midst of my stomach; just like rivers of living waters as it said in JOHN 7:37 In the last day, that great day of the feast, Jesus stood and cried, saying, If any man thirst, let him come unto me, and drink 38

He that believeth on me, as the scripture hath said, out of his belly shall flow rivers of living water 39 (But this spoke he of the Spirit, which they that believe on him should receive: for the Holy Spirit was not yet given; because that Jesus was not yet glorified). ACTS 2: 4 and when the day of Pentecost was fully come; they were all with one accord in one place. 2 And suddenly there came a sound from heaven as of a rushing mighty wind, and it filled the house where they were sitting. 3. And there appeared unto them cloven tongues like as of fire, and it sat upon each of them. 4 And they were all filled with the Holy Spirit, and began to speak with other tongues, as the Spirit gave them utterance. (Language)

After about a couple of hours we would go our separate ways until the next Saturday. When I arrived home, I would get my bible, notebook and my index cards with passages of scriptures written on them and start memorizing scriptures, while listening to a tape which I had recorded from one of our church worship and preaching or bible and history teachings, when we were having bible study on Saturday night at my folks home or one of the other Christians home and on Sunday we would rent a building in Charlotte and Albion Michigan, which was twenty and forty miles from Lansing, Michigan where I lived. (I did not mind the distance to receive the teaching that I received I could not get it anywhere else except from one of our other Gospel Assemble Churches which were located in other States.

I did not have a church home for about six months after I received the baptism of the Holy Spirit on September 5, 1972 with the evidence of speaking in a heavenly language. And I received the baptism of water a couple years later at one of our Church conventions in Saint Louis, Missouri by being placed underneath the water exactly like they did in the bible in 1 PETER 3:21 The like figure where unto even baptism doth also now save us (not the putting a way of the filth of the flesh, but answer of a good conscience toward God, by the resurrection of Jesus Christ. Peter was explaining that water baptism saves us but has nothing to do with Spiritual baptism by speaking in a heavenly language; but it does save us because it's a good conscience toward God because we did what was commanded of us to do to complete that phase of our salvation. In the Law of Moses, it was natural circumcision but under the grace covenant it was Spiritual baptism with the evidence of speaking in a heavenly language.

During the times I was fasting, I felt such a power and anointing from the Holy Spirit that would over shadow me with a great love, that prepared me to continue to have a great love for Jesus and God the Father and my love for them continued to grow stronger each day and I looked forward to praying and witnessing on my job at General

Motors and I was on the assembly line working very hard and every day when the relief person would relief me I would find myself a very quiet place so I could memorize the scriptures that I had placed on index cards and I would always carry my small pocket bible in my shirt pocket; so, everyone would know that I was a Born-Again Christian in the Non-Denominational Pentecostal Faith. I started my Christian life in serving the Lord Jesus on September 5, 1972, as a young single man and after receiving the Baptism of the Holy Spirit in a Revival in the Lansing, Michigan area, and my brother-in-law Evangelist John C. Quinn would come to Lansing to run revivals and others would come to help him and they were from the Bay area in San Francisco.

He's the Evangelist that chose me to be the President of the Deliverance Crusaders a witness group that was formed after the Revival that I received the wonderful gift of the Holy Spirit, which is the life of God; because God is a Spiritual eternal being of pure energy with no beginning or ending of days, and Jesus His beloved Son was created for man-kind but when it's all said and done the angel shall declare that time shall be no more REVELATION 22:3. I would take a vacation to Richman California before I changed my life and became a Christian and after becoming a Christian I would visit my sister that's next to me who was Saved and Filled with the precious Gift of the Holy Spirit in San Pablo, California.

I would sometime take a vacation during changeover at General Motors during the summer and again during the Christmas Holidays which usually was for about two weeks, and sometimes I would extend the time by taking vacation time; so, I could help my brother-in-law run Revivals and what an experience and that's one of the reasons why I love witnessing to people about Jesus who will be King of Kings and Lord of Lords when he comes back for the bride of Jesus Christ which is a special people that has satisfied the mind of God that they could live throughout the seedless ages of eternity and never commit another sin or be a security risk.

Those trips really inspired and encouraged me to seek more of Jesus in my life, that I would continue to grow and abound in the work of the Lord Jesus; and many times, he would be running Revivals at a church in Berkeley, Oakland and Saint Francisco, California. And he would always let the people know how Jesus had filled me with his Holy Spirit and Brother Elmo was Lansing, Michigan District "Boxer of the Year' and the zeal and enthusiasm he have for the love of Christ by giving out his tracts for witnessing with his boxing picture on it and the word 'Boxer of the Year' And the way he testified about what Jesus is doing in his life and the scriptures he has memorized quoting the book, chapter, and verse. My brother-in-law had a radio station where he came on each week in Saint Francisco, California and then he would have me to give my testimony. And he was an Evangelist in The Church of God in Christ in Berkeley California where Bishop Cleveland was the overseer and was known all over the world. He would always amaze me with the strong faith he had in calling people out to be Saved, Sanctified, and Filled with the Holy Spirit and healed, delivered and set free by the power of the Holy Spirit. I used to marvel of all the young and old people would move out of their seats and come up to the altar to be prayed for and afterwards some of them would give their testimony that would be broadcast live from San Francisco radio studio. The people received the Holy Spirit exactly like they received it on the day of Pentecost with the evidence of speaking in a heavenly language as the Spirit give them utterance as it said in ACTS 2:4 And they were all filled with the Holy Spirit and begin to speak in other tongues (Languages) as the Spirit gave them utterance. I was so impressed how the Holy Spirit would come upon the people that the God of heaven and earth, The creator of the universe through His son Jesus Christ who was on earth for thirty three and a half years and was humiliated and scorn and beaten and hung on a cross to die and afterwards place in a tomb for three days and nights in Jewish time and rose triumph from the tomb to live forever more.

It had to be three days because the number three is a biblical number which stands for perfection and when you see a number in a scripture many times you can know what a scripture means by the number that is applied to the setting. In ST. JOHN 16:7 Nevertheless I tell you the truth: It is expedient for you that I go away: for if I go not away, the comforter will not come unto you: but if I depart, I will send him unto you. When Jesus was here on earth he was their comforter, now he's in heaven sitting down at the right hand of his Father 'JEHOVAH' "GOD". Then he sent us another comforter in the form of the Holy Spirit that Jesus received from his Father and to all others who obey him God himself who is a Spirit being and He is eternal with no beginning or ending of days for He is life himself.

I Thank God that I have life within this earthly house in the form of the Holy Spirit who God gives to all those who will receive it, and it is just as strong in my life as it was from the beginning of my Spirit filled life; since September 5, 1972. I was filled with the Holy Spirit six years while a single young man and was blessed with my wife 'Cathie 'Cobb' Hudson and we have three children two boys and a girl, Eric Linn Hudson, Alaina Marie Hudson, and Steven Michael Hudson and all three have Bachelor's degrees, Eric graduated from Ferris State University with a degree in Criminal Justice in 2013. And Alaina graduated from Atlanta Clark University in Georgia with a degree in Marketing in 2001.

And Steven graduated from Michigan State University with a degree in Marketing in 2012. We were married on July 15, 1978. And my wife Cathie Ann 'Cobb' Hudson received her Associate Degree at Lansing Community College and her Bachelor degree in Business at Eastern Michigan University and received her Master degree on a Sabbatical leave at Michigan State University, while teaching at Lansing Community College and she was asked while attending Eastern Michigan University if she would like to teach at Lansing Community College she retired as a full Professor. I love being a Christian in the Non-Denominational Pentecostal Church; because I was led there by Divine Revelation and we work as a section of The Body of Christ among ourselves and we trace our church from the day of Pentecost with the divine teaching of the God Gifted and sent Apostles.

I admired Jesus in the way he paved the way for Man-Kind by setting the standard we are to attain to by the life he lived. In 1 Peter 2:21-25 for even here unto were ye called; because Christ also suffered for us leaving us an example, that ye should follow his steps. 22 who did no sin, neither was guile found in his mouth. 23 who when he was reviled, reviled not again; when he suffered he threatened not; but committed himself to him that Judgeth righteously. 24 who his own self bears our sins in his own body on the tree, that we, being dead to sins, should live unto righteousness; by whose stripes ye were healed. 25 for ye were as sheep going astray, but are now returned unto the Shepherd and Bishop of your souls. And Jesus is the person that I follow and I have pattern my life after him in every aspect of my life, and I am still in training and have continued to be taught through the Ministry in our section of the Body of Christ, and we are all taught and instructed in righteousness and we all believe the same doctrinal teachings of Jesus and the God Gifted Apostle's in the early reign church with the true teachings and interpretations of the scriptures.

The God who created the heaven's and earth has blessed us with knowledge that has been hid from the masses and we are a people that love the word of God and we are preparing ourselves to live eternally on the New Earth with a number that no human being can count, which just means a multiplicity of people. In the final analysis of the plan of God there will be more people on top of the earth for eternity than those that are dead and underneath the earth. I love Holiness, Righteousness, Perfection, and an overcoming life to be like Christ. All of our churches believe the same doctrinal teachings the Apostles taught two thousand years ago in Jerusalem and planted churches in the known world in there day. All our churches have continued to advance with knowledge and wisdom of everything that pertain to life and godliness. And because Jesus led me to a people that he called out to preach and teach the true gospel, which has blessed me with a zeal and enthusiasm that has produce ripe fruit in my life by applying those truth to my life so people can see the Christ that live in me that has continued to prepare me for an eternal existence.

The events and happenings in the Holy Bible that's yet to be fulfilled, but I believe through the things that I have observed lately is right on time to fulfill the scriptures that has been written in the prophesies and in the book of Revelations, which most church going people don't have any knowledge of, but will hear God Gifted Apostles, Prophets, Evangelists, Preachers and Teachers, for the perfection of the Saints, and for the work of the Ministry and for the edifying of the 'Body of Christ' till we all come in the unity of the faith and of the knowledge of the Son of God unto a perfect man, unto the measure of the stature of the fullness of Christ. This scripture is yet to be fulfilled in EPHESIANS 4:11-13; But those scriptures will come to life just prior to the coming of Christ, when God will manifest himself one more time to justify him in destroying this world at the battle of Armageddon in Revelation 16:16 And he gathered them together into a place called in the Hebrew tongue Armageddon.

I remember after a few months without a church home and I was so tired of hearing the same message over and over and the people did not seem very friendly so I started staying home and studying the bible and memorizing the scriptures and on Saturdays and during the weekdays I would continue to witness for Christ in endeavoring to win lost souls to the kingdom of God. After the Deliverance Crusaders witness group dropped off one by one till I was the only one left being the President of the group. I looked at it this way; since I am the captain of the ship then it was my job to be the last one to vacate the ship in the time of storm or turmoil and forty-three years later. I am still aboard the ship and that which holds the ship in place is the anchor and I am attach firmly to Jesus Christ, the anchor of my soul.

I also continued to go to Alcohol Anonymous meetings to witness to the lost and dying, and I would go to the highway safety meetings at Saint Lawrence Hospital to witness to those there that had lost their license on drunk driving charges and had to go through the program before reapplying for their driver's license, and I had lost my license for ninety days and placed on three years' probation prior to changing my life in becoming a Born Again Christian in the Non-Denominational Pentecostal Faith. I was told I had to go through the program in order to get my license reinstated I explained to the clerk that I had changed my life and had no desire to live the life I once had lived he did not understand and said he think I still should go I said I can't and I went home and prayed to the Lord Jesus and explain to him the circumstances to him; then I went to apply again and the clerk looked unsure about me; since I had not gone through the program; but he reinstated my license and I thank Jesus for intervening in my behalf as a young man in Christ.

I later started going to the prison ministry at Riverside Correction Facility in Ionia Michigan for the youths (with 'O'Neil and May Carter who went to the Christian Reform Church in East Lansing across from Michigan State University who were in charge of the meeting's) until they were twenty-one years of age, then they would send them to an adult prison'. They eventually closed this facility so I prayed the prayer of faith that the Lord would open up another prison so I could continue as a volunteer. Then someone from The Christian Reform Church in East Lansing got in touch with me that they were going to another prison in Ionia called Bellamy Creek Correction Facility who Richard and Carol Riestra was the pastor and piano player who was with The Christian Reform Church in Grand Rapids and later he started working with returning Citizens Alliance who provided assisted to prisoners that had served their time and was released to those programs that provided housing, clothing and jobs for them.

Then Reverend Andy Hanson took over and the meetings were called Celebration Fellowship which I am still attending as a volunteer but I am of the Non-Denominational Pentecostal Faith but the Lord Jesus open the door for me to go after much prayer. I learned through experience the more I fasted, and let the word of God assimilate, digest and become part of me, and by praying before I go to bed at night and when I get up in the mornings and the more I reach out in worshipping and praising the Lord Jesus the Holy Spirit becomes stronger and stronger and I would exercise the Holy Spirit by speaking in a heavenly language and the tears, and crying with joy and The Spirit moving me so powerful and it was great. I felt that whatever I pray for in the will of God's Son would come to fruition with joy unspeakable and full of glory. In the book of JOHN 7:37, 38, 39 in the last day, that great day of the feast, Jesus stood and cried, If any man thirst, let him come unto me, and drink. 38 He that believeth on me, as the scripture hath said. Out of his belly shall flow rivers of living water. 39 But this spoke he of the

Spirit, which they that believe on him should receive, for the Holy Spirit was not yet given, because that Jesus was not yet glorified. I felt when I would pray every night before going to bed and then reaching out to the Lord Jesus in worship and praising the Holy Spirit would overshadow me with a great love, with clouds of joy like a fountain of living water inside the midst of my stomach with tears of joy and I would continue to praise him while the rivers of living water were blessing me with joy unspeakable and full of glory.

Then in the morning when I would pray that God through His Son Jesus would forgive me for any sins that I might have committed, and anything in my life that's not Christ like, then I would pray to the Lord and the Holy Spirit would began to move me and it is still with me. In the book of HEBREWS 13: 5 let your conversation be without covetousness; and be content with such things as ye have: for He hath said, I will never leave thee, nor forsake thee. And that scripture is the reason why the Holy Spirit is still with me. There's another scripture that said in 1 Timothy 2:5 for there is one God, and one mediator between God and men, the man Christ Jesus.

In JOHN 17:11 and now I am no more in the world, but these are in the world, and I come to thee, Holy Father, keep through thy own name those whom thou has given me that they may be one, as we are. In Ephesians 5: 23 for the husband is the head of his wife, even as Christ is the head of the church: and he is the savior of the body. The reason I used the name Jesus instead of His Father 'Jehovah' God is because Jesus is the head of the church. In ACTS 4:12 neither is there salvation in any other: for there is none other name under heaven given among men, whereby we must be saved 'JESUS' I have always kept the Holy Spirit active in my life, by obeying the word of God. When I was single I lived on the same street as my folks in one of their rental houses. I became a Christian while living in my parent's rental house and I also live there after the Lord blessed me with my wife. I lived a Holy life and that's all I knew because that was how I was taught and research those scriptures as we were instructed by our individual pastors.

I depended solely on the Holy Spirit for the zeal that I have had, continually for the Lord. I remember after I became a Born-Again

Christian in a Revival at Robinson Memorial Church of God in Christ in Lansing, Michigan conducted by Evangelist John C. Quinn and His wife Jesterine and the Deliverance Crusaders from the Bay Area in Berkeley and Oakland California. I visit several Pentecostal churches and went to many Revivals and in those days they really had some good Evangelists. I have never became a member of any church I just attend, because in the book of ACTS 2: 47 Praising God, and having favor with all the people. And the Lord added to the church daily such as should be saved. I have been taught if God adds you to His church then you don't have to be voted in or become a member because if you have a genuine love for truth then they will continue to come and become part of our fellowship or part of our section of the Body of Christ.

I finally was tired of pastors preaching basically the same sermon each time that I would visit a church and the people weren't very friendly. I finally decided that I would just continue to study and witness to the unsaved as I always did on my job at General Motors or whenever the opportunity avail itself and on Saturday after praying the prayer of faith and praising the Lord and the Holy Spirit confirming that Jesus was pleased with me going out knocking on doors and witnessing to people and in my own neighborhood and walking and standing downtown Lansing passing out my tracts and placing the information on telephone poles that the Deliverance Crusaders were coming to the city to hold a Revival. After about a Month not attending a church my father Lacy Hudson called me and said it's not good to stay at home and invited me to visit their church?

I accepted the invitation and visit their Church 'they had services on Thursday and Saturday nights and Sunday they had morning Sunday school, then they would move into the afternoon service and then between service they would dismiss for dinner and came back for Sunday evening services at seven o'clock'. I knew the pastor Fred Young and his wife Joann was white and the whole congregation except my parents, Aunt Beatrice Clement and a friend of theirs Bessie Summerville.

We were all born and raised in the south around Gurdon and Springhill, Arkansas where I also was born, we moved north when

I was about four years old. I was so impressed with their service and how the pastor could teach the word of God and bring the scriptures together in their correct sequence and order and I knew it was correct and he did not have to read from his bible and all was done by memory and I said to myself this makes sense this is what I have been looking for and after the service I met the pastor and the other Christians I was so grateful that my father had invited me to visit their church and I was praying and waiting that he would call me again, and invite me to their church. I continued to study the bible and memorize the scriptures etc…After several weeks in not attending a church my father called me again and basically said the same words that it is not good to stay at home why don't you visit our church again? I told him I would and my prayer had been answered and I have continued to come and believe this teaching of Gospel Assembly Non-Denominational Pentecostal Churches.

I remember one scripture that really stood out the pastor was teaching and quoted I PETER 2:21-25 for even hereunto were ye called: because Christ also suffered for us, leaving us an example, that ye should follow his steps. 22 who did no sin, neither was guile found in his mouth: 23. who when he was reviled, reviled not again; when he suffered, he threatened not; but committed himself to him that judgeth righteously: 24 who his own self bare our sins in his own body on the tree that we, being dead to sins, should live unto righteousness: by whose stripes ye were healed. 25 for ye were as sheep going astray; but are now returned unto the Shepherd and Bishop of your souls. Then in HEBREW 2: 16-17. For verily he took not on him the nature of angels; but he took on him the seed of Abraham. 17. Wherefore in all things it behooved him to be made like unto his brethren, that he might be a merciful and faithful high priest in things pertaining to God, to make reconciliation for the sins of the people.

He said Abraham became the father of the Jewish nation through Jacob and his twelve sons, and the Jews are God's chosen people, and in the seventh day the gospel will go back into the hand of God's chosen people in the seventh day, which is a thousand year day. And 2 PETER 3: 8 but beloved be not ignorant of this one thing, that one day with the Lord is a thousand years, and a thousand years as one day. In Hosea 6:1-2 come and let us return to the Lord: for He had torn, and He will heal us, He had smitten, and He will bind us up. 2 After two day's will he revive us, in the third day He will raise us up, and we shall live in his sight. And then he said God cut the Jewish nation off for two days which he said was two thousand years, from Adam to Christ and from Christ to the end of this two thousand years will be six thousand years, and the third day will be the seventh thousand year, which would be the third year from when Christ came until the end of the third day. There is six days in a week and the seventh day God rested from all His works which God created and made.

He also told the congregation the importance of numbers, which have pacific functions and meaning to interpret the scriptures and everything in the bible is in sequence and in order. Then he opened the service up for the people to give their testimony to edify one another, in Psalms, Proverb's and Hymns and Spiritual songs. And most of the testimony's was about striving for perfection to become an over comer and it was not an option it was necessary and vital for Jesus was our example who did no sin, neither was guile found in His mouth. The thing that was really unite we work among ourselves as a section of The Body of Christ and we do not ask others for help in any form shade of variation and the knowledge and understanding they have of the order of God and the interpretation of the scriptures is great and they can prove everything we are taught by them and that in itself is outstanding and there cannot be any contradiction with another scripture or interpretation.

Here's some of the Spiritual literature our churches put together and they are distributed to the congregations. (SING UNTO THE LORD A NEW SONG) When words fail to express the exalted sentiments and finer thing of the human heart, music becomes the language of the soul, the divine instrumentality for its higher utterance. Each of your friends has his principles melody. It is not what he says or does now and then that is most important. IT IS THE MELODY THAT COMES FROM HIS WHOLE LIFE! Here is another of our work that our churches put together (CHRIST IS RISEN) Hallelujah! He is raised!

Christ is raised from the dead Oh, behold the man immortal! He is raised, as He said cross or grave could not retain Him raging foe nor piercing sound. He is now the mighty conqueror, Hallelujah! Praise the Lord! Hallelujah! He is raised! Christ's is raised from the grave. He that was so meek and lowly stands there mighty now to save. Heavenly portals standing open, Bring to view the throne of God, where He lives and reigns forever. Hallelujah! Praise the Lord! Hallelujah! He is raised! Christ is raised; come and bring Glory to our precious Savior, Son of God, our Lord and King. Every tongue shall soon confess Him; every knee before Him bow, and the world shall see His glory, Hallelujah! Praise the Lord. (FOR HE IS NOT HERE: FOR HE IS RISEN, AS HE SAID: COME SEE THE PLACE WHERE THE LORD LAY) MATTHEW 28:6.

Here's another of our well thought out teachings: (RESURRECTION POWER EVERY DAY) that I may know him, and the power of his resurrection, and the fellowship of his sufferings, being made conformable unto his death. PHILLIPIANS 3:10. Some of us wait at the tomb, quicken and risen together with Christ; yet linger still in its gloom, some of us abide at the Passover Feast with Pentecost all unknown: The triumphs of grace in the Heavenly place that our Lord has made our own. If the Christ who died had stopped at the cross, His work had been incomplete; if the Christ who was buried had stated in the tomb He had only know defeat. But the way of the cross never stops at the cross, and the way of the tomb leads on to victorious grace in the Heavenly Place, where the risen Lord has gone.

Here's another of our great works (CHRIST ALONE) the world, I thought, belonged to me goods, gold and people, land and sea, wherever I walked beneath God's sky in those old days my word was 'I'; years passed, there flashed my pathway near. The fragment of a vision dear; my former word no more sufficed. And what I said was – I had Christ." But, O the more I looked on Him, His glory grew, while mine grew dim; I shrank so small. He tower so High, All I dared say was –Christ and I. Years passed the vision held its place and looked me steadily in the face; I speak now in humbler tone, and what I say is – Christ alone.

Here's another with has great Spiritual significance and well put together (WRECKERS AND BUILDERS): I watched them tearing a building down – A gang of men in a big town, with a heave ho and a lusty yell, they swung a beam and the sidewall fell, I asked the foreman, "Are these men skilled? The kind you would hire if you wanted to build: He laughed and said "Why, no indeed, just labor, common labor, is all I need. They can easily wreck in a day or two, what builders have taking years to do. I asked myself as I went my way, which of these roles have I played today? As a builder who works with care measuring life by ruling square? Shaping my deeds by the vertical place, or am I the wreck that lost the town beset with the labor of tearing down?

Here's to all that wants to be important (ALL V.I.P.'S) All have a share in the beauty, all have a part in the plan, what does it matter what duty falls to the lot of man? Someone must blend the plaster and someone must carry the stone, neither the man nor master, even has built alone. Making a roof from the weather, or building a house for a king, only by working together have men ever accomplished a thing. Here's another that's really impressive (HOW CHRIST IS EXPRESSED) not merely in the words you say, not only in your deeds confessed, but in the most unconscious way is Christ expressed. For me was not the truth you taught, to you so clear, to me so dim, but when you came to me you brought a sense of him, and from your eyes He beckons me, and from your heart his love is shed, till I lose sight of me and see the Christ instead. Jesus said in MATTHEW 7:14 because strait is the gate, and narrow is the way, which leadeth unto life, and few there be that find it. 9 (THE EASY ROAD CROWDED) The easy roads are crowded and the level roads are jammed; The pleasant little rivers with the drifting folds are crammed, but off yonder where its rocky the ranks are thinning and the travelers are few, when the going's smooth and pleasant, you will always find the throng, for the many, more the pity seem to like to drift along; and the task that's hard to do, in the end results in glory for the never wavering few. These are a few of the great poems and

Proverbs that our section of the 'Body of Christ' connected together and they are scriptural, and doctrinal sound.

I said after hearing these beautiful heavenly words this is it this sounds like what Jesus and the Apostles taught and I listen to the songs and how they played the organ, piano and other music instruments. I said to myself the songs did not sound that good and the way they play their music because I was used to hearing the music instruments and the songs played and song differently than I had been accustomed to hearing in Church of God in Christ. After the service I drove home and turned on a cassette player and I listened to Evangelist and the music and songs and the Testimony's from the 'BLACK' Churches of God and Christ. I continued to fast, pray and praise the Lord and going out witnessing by myself during the week days and on Saturday's in Downtown Lansing, Michigan and pass out my 'Boxer of the Year' Tracts with my U.S. ARMY picture on the front page, when I was on the Third Army Boxing Team at Fort McClellan in Anniston, Alabama. I was the 126-pound featherweight boxing champion and our boxing team went to Fort Campbell Kentucky for the Third Army Boxing Tournament, where I was nominated for the All Army Boxing Team).

After about three weeks after visiting Gospel Assembly Church and not attending a church since then. My Father called me again and basically said the same identical words, it's not good to stay at home, come and visit our church again and that was all I wanted to hear and I went and have been going ever since. I analyze the church situation and came to the conclusion the most important aspect of the service is the great teaching who can explain the scripture and can prove with other scriptures truth in the inward part. This was the only church we had, in the Capital City of Michigan. We were taught the early church had only one church in a city that was operating with the Five Gifted Ministry in EPHESIANS 4:11-13 and he gave some, Apostles; and some, Prophets: and some Evangelists: and some: Pastors, and Teachers: 12 for the perfecting of the saints, for the work of the ministry, for the edifying of the body of Christ: 13 till we all come in the unity of the faith, and of the knowledge of the

Son of God, unto a perfect man, unto the measure of the stature of the fullness of Christ:

I have been taught if we don't have more to offer than other churches in the city, then we need to join them, for there are many churches in Lansing, Michigan which have small congregations. He also said that with the understanding of no church in any city have the knowledge and wisdom of understanding the scriptures as our Pastors and Ministers who have dedicated their life since the founding of our churches in 1913 and have continued to work in striving to be one in Him 'Jesus' we will be; as it is written in ST. JOHNS 17:11 And now I am no more in the world, but these are in the world, and I come to thee, Holy Father keep through thy own name those whom thou hast given me, that they may be one, as we are. How are God and his Son Jesus one, just like in EPHESIANS 5:31-32 for this cause shall a man leave his father and mother, and shall be joined unto his wife, and they two shall be one flesh. 32 this is a great mystery: but I speak concerning Christ and the church. Then he would say, just like a husband and wife is one; yet they are two different persons, yet they are one.

We were having church services in a church, when the Lord sent me there and we were there for about a year when our pastor decided we needed to move out of the neighborhood and it was not long after then the church was sold to a Apostolic African American congregation. We had some great services the short time I was there and the teaching was the best I have ever heard and everything had to be done decently and in order and the church was immaculate. I also notice there were no joking or foolish talking or jesting, and when someone misquoted a scripture or tripped over a rug, and almost fall, most people would have given in to the human nature and start laughing and they came to church with their minds girded up in spiritual inspiration, and they did not believe in telling jokes of any kind especially those that were demeaning to bring Christ down on their level.

I also notice how they behave and conducted themselves before, during and after the services. They had been taught and school in the ways of the Lord. I also notice the women wore dresses with long sleeves and their hair was fixed in a certain style and the young girls could wear their hair down until a certain age then they had to wear their hair up as the older women in the church. The men conducted themselves in the same manner in having to wear a suit, white shirt and tie, and their hair had to be cut short and clean shaved or if they had a mustache, they had to have it trimmed neatly. The children were very mannerly and respectful to the elders or older saints and some of the younger people played in the band and they were students of the bible in that they were taught in children, teenager and adult Sunday school classes and they were taught how to live a Christian life and represent Christ as a positive role model; so, the world could see the examples of Christ and the Apostles teachings in us and they place emphasis in portraying Christ in their life.

I like to hear how Christ taught and instructed his disciples and followers. It was not an option with us to follow the examples set by Jesus Christ to prepare us for eternity, to live on the new earth throughout the seedless and endless ages of eternity. In PSALMS 78:69 and he built his sanctuary like high palaces, like the earth which he has established forever; so the earth will always be here and the curse will be lifted off the earth in REVELATIONS 22:3 and there shall be no more curse: but the throne of God and of the Lamb shall be in it: and his servants shall serve him. Then it will be a beautiful paradise, and circumstances and conditions will be changed there will be a new form of Government set up; so everything will be new in that respect. In EPHESIANS 5:26-27 that he might sanctify and cleanse it with the washing of water by the word. 27 that he might present it to himself a glorious church, not having spot, or wrinkle, or any such thing: but that it should be holy and without blemish.

Everything is on a time table, so everything has to happen in the time frame of God's eternal plan to bring in the inauguration of the latter rain church, to get the remaining o His bride from the early reign church. Then after the bride is taking up into third heaven which was a type of the Tabernacle in the wilderness, where there were three compartments. The first compartment which was symbolic of the Gentiles and it had red curtains that divided it from the second compartment which had purple curtains symbolizing of

Jesus called the Holy place dividing it from the third compartment called the Holy of Holy's and it was draped in blue curtains which was where the present of God dwell. The red curtains was a type of this sinful world and mix God's color with it, which blue and you get purple which is Jesus color. In 1 TIMOTHY 2: 5 for there is one God, and one mediator between God and man, the man Christ Jesus, so he can take our prayers and those petitions before God His Father. The religious leaders in the time of Jesus said he make himself as God and poked fun at him and took a purple robe and placed on him, in ridiculing him, why did they not place a blue robe on him for they said Jesus said He was God; and God's color is blue? They place a purple robe on him and fulfill the scripture that Jesus is not God but he is the son of God.

I love the order of God and he does everything according to His divine plan with everything set in order. I love our churches for it is the agency of God's salvation, for mankind. It is the expression of the love of God as it is revealed in Jesus Christ our Lord. Our churches seeks to build the kingdom of God, beginning here and now; It seeks to do God's will on earth as it is in heaven. Our church is composed of human beings, just sinners saved by grace. It has no perfect people, but it seeks to make them so. It offers no easy living. Rather it challenges us to venture forth to live for God in the Spirit of Jesus Christ. Our church needs us and we need our churches for this is the means God uses to carry forward His redemptive work-through human beings, who are His own creation. (WE LOVE OUR CHURCH)!

(OUR MINISTER): He is love in action, love with its hand to the plow, love with the burden on its back, love following in the footsteps of our Lord, who went about doing good continually. The proud he tame, the penitent he cheers; nor to rebuke the offender, does he fear; he preaches much, but more His practice-wrought, a living sermon of the truths he taught. He does not ask that men may sound His praise, or headline spread his name abroad he only asks that as he voices his message... HEARTS MAY FIND GOD! Music and Singing and Worshiping have always played a great part in building up our church.

(HEAVENLY FATHER, WE COME BEFORE YOUR ETERNAL THRONE) with this petition, that we, as musicians, might fulfill our calling in producing harmonious tones which will cause your people to lift their hearts to the utmost heights of true worship. We want to produce harmony that the Holy Spirit provides into our Assembly in such a divine way, that it will change the life of every person that is present for that worship service. We desire to produce 'MUSIC' that will bring the sinner to his knees in sincere repentance before God. 'MUSIC' that will thrill the souls of those that already experienced the resurrection power of salvation. 'MUSIC' that will bring your energizing power into our midst to healed the afflicted, maimed and blind; 'MUSIC' that will draw heaven so close that you can inspire the teaching of the everlasting plan of redemption in its completeness, so that souls can go all the way to perfection once again.

We know that if we, the musicians of the 'Body of Christ' ever aspire to the vision that is set before us by our ministry, we must bring our lives in harmony with your great order. We must work in according with the minister, the music staff and the saints of God, so that no discord will come between us to hinder your work; but our spirits will be in harmonious love which will flow from one heart to the other. We want to inspire everyone to blend their spirits, as well as their voices, together when they play and sing. When everyone in the congregation blends their voices together, may it be the greatest sound this world has ever heard. O' God, we know that heaven's first discord was cause by one that became exalted because of his musical ability. May we always realize that every talent you have given us is to be used in giving honor and glory back to you, we long to see that true worship, which requires a perfect blend of our Spirits and Voices, so that the voices from the angelic realm will harmonize with ours in perfect WORSHIP and adoration to you – Our Creator, Lord and King, Grant that we may fully fulfilled our mission in bringing harmony back to earth again and that we may be used in RESTORING A GLORIOUS CHURCH.

I will sing of the Mercies of the Lord Forever: With my mouth will I make known thy Faithfulness to all Generations PSALMS

89:1. I have continued to stand up for the Kingdom of God's sake and portray Christ in my life the Son of the most high God, and when I was led by the Holy Spirit to do a certain thing that I had prayed for and it would happen and I have always kept the faith, nobody has had any greater influence in my life than the Son of God, Jesus Christ.

My whole life and being has been devoted to him and I believed God for everything, and I would always seek him in prayer and to feel the Holy Spirit, which is the life of God, moving me like the wind blowing, but cannot tell whither its coming or going, but you know it's there for you can see it blowing the leaves and bushes just so nice and smooth and in contrast it does to everything that's pliable. Jesus said to Nicodemus ruler of the Jews. In John 3:1-3 THERE was a man of the Pharisees, named Nicodemus, a ruler of the Jews. 2 the same came to Jesus by night, and said unto him, Rabbi, we know that thou art a teacher come from God: For no man can do these miracles that thou do, except God be with him. 3 Jesus answered and said unto him, verily, verily, I say unto thee, except a man be born again, he cannot see the kingdom of God. 4 Nicodemus said unto him, how can a man be born when he is old? Can he enter the second time into his mother's womb, and be born?

5. Jesus answered, verily, verily, I unto thee, except a man be born of the water of the Spirit, he cannot enter into the Kingdom of God. 6. That which is born of the flesh is flesh; and that which is born of the Spirit is Spirit. 7 Marvel not that I said unto thee, ye must be born again. 8 the wind bloweth where it listeth, and thou hearest the sound thereof, but canst not tell whence it cometh, and whither it goeth, so is everyone that is born of the Spirit. 9 Nicodemus answered and said unto him, art thou a master of Israel and newest not these things? 11. Verily, verily, I say unto thee, we speak that we do know, and testify that we have seen; and ye receive not our witness 12 if I have told you earthly things, and ye believe not, how shall you believe, if I tell you of heavenly things? 13 and no man hath ascended up to heaven, but he that came down from heaven, even the son of man, which is in heaven. This scripture was said by John thirty years after Jesus hath ascended up into heaven, that's why it's so important to know when

the books of the bible was written. Someone told our founder; who God called to the Ministry and gave him so many truths of the bible; that's been hid from most of the religion leaders of our day.

This pastor told him this scripture proves that God and Jesus is the same person; that he was in heaven and earth at the same time? Our Founder who God called by Devine Revelation, and instructed him to preach my gospel. The Holy Spirit gave him the answer, this was John telling them about Jesus and not Jesus doing the talking, for he had been in heaven for thirty years, when John made that statement, so it's necessary to study who is during the talking and what time frame the book was written. The Holy Bible is our only love letter from God and we should love it enough to learn how to study the bible by seeking the truth. And God cannot condone falsehood or untruth. Every scripture has to be place in its right sequence or order; for there to be no contradiction to the other scriptures, in seeking the pure unadulterated word of God. The revelation we received on how to study the books of the bible, ask ourselves these five questions? When; what, where, Why and How and then we would find out how to unravel those great truths, that has been hidden from the masses and giving to God's chosen few.

And that is why I am so blessed to have a Devine Revelation from God, that these are the people God has open these great truths that has been hid from the masses, and giving to God's chosen few. That's why I am so blessed to have a Devine Revelation from God, that these are the people He has open the bible refers to as the hidden ones. The Ministers and laity copy or repeat what other ministers are saying about a certain scripture, not knowing if its correct or not just as long as it sound good and the different tactics they used to make themselves seem more spiritual than the congregations by throwing a piece of cloth and it hitting someone and the person start acting like the spirit is upon them and that type of manifestation brings a reproach upon the Pentecostal people and it affects other groups of people and they know it's not of God, but just deceiving the people to make themselves out as some great one.

I have also seen in visiting other churches lately Ministers praying for the people and speaking in other tongues which is a heavenly language when done properly, but I am afraid that many Pentecostal churches are playing church. They have lost the power that they had when God called there founder to established those churches at the turn of the early nineteen hundreds, when God start working with the Pentecostal movement that has split into different groups with different doctrinal teachings and has lost their first love in 2 TIMOTHY 3:5 having a form of Godliness, but denying the power thereof: from such turn away.

They are two will's mention in the bible that govern our Christian life in applying the word of God to our lives and that is God permissive will; which is when He allows things to happen but not necessarily condoning it and God's perfect will is doing exactly what God would have an individual to do. I have found out in my experience in striving for perfection in doing everything require for us to do in the bible, cannot be accomplish unless I am seeking truth and truth means being able to accept truth from whoever God gives it to, and many organizations have refused to accept truth unless it comes from their organization, therefore they are still holding on to same truth God gave to their founder and will not accept the truth God has giving to other faiths. We understand how God is working and we have search other organization truths that God had gave their movement and we have accepted that truths and has advance and moved on in the word of God.

There has been many of God's people He has dispense truth to; but they have fail to receive truth from any source God has giving it to; as a result of their refusal to accept truth only if it came from their organization, and many of movements have made that same mistake; which has caused God to move on to somebody else or raise somebody up that would accept truth from any source God would give it to. And God has done that with our section of the Body of Christ. We have study the doctrines of other faiths and have accepted their truth, with the truth God has given us. The Body of Christ, which is not separated and divided. The truth must be taught and not compromise to please people, whether people accept it now or later, it still have to be taught. God will not accept false teaching every person that is saved from their pass sins or fill with the Holy Spirit will have to have the truth taught to them at the final resurrection and they will have the choice to accept or reject the truth that has been taught by the God Gifted Ministry.

There can be only one gospel and one truth; every person has to be one in Christ. The Body of Christ is not separated and divided. In DANIEL 7:22 until the Ancient of days came, and judgment was given to the saints of the most High; and the time came that the saints possessed the kingdom. He had this vision and God let him see what was going too happened when most people cannot see this happening, but Daniel said the time came that the saints possess the Kingdom. Those that God has giving that Revelation to will be prepared; when the cry goes forth in 2 CORINTHIAN 6:16-18 and what agreement hath the temple of God with idols? For you are the temple of living God; as God hath said, I will dwell in them, and walk in them; and I will be there God, and they shall be my people. 17 wherefore come out from among them and be ye separated, said the lord, and touch not the unclean thing, and I will receive you. 18 and will be a father to you and you shall be my sons and daughters, said the Lord Almighty.

And in 2 CORINTHIANS 7:1 having therefore, these promises, dearly beloved let us cleanse ourselves from all filthiness of the flesh and Spirit, perfecting holiness in the fear of the God. Then in REVELATION 18:4 and I heard another voice from heaven, saying, come out of her my people, that you be not partakers of her sins, and that your receive not of her plagues. When the cry comes forth; come out of her my people; there has to be a section of the 'Body of Christ' for them to go into, to be taught whatever is lacking in their life to prepare them for an eternal existence. This also shows a Spiritual birth can take place in any Church but in the final analysis they still have to be able to hear and accept the truth in order to make up the Bride of Christ in the first resurrection and live a thousand years in heaven before the last resurrection and eventually live throughout the seedless and endless ages of eternity on the new earth with God and His beloved Son Jesus Christ.

When an individual goes to a church that is not being taught the truth when it is open up to them the bible talks about many subjects and deals with many facets of life. Therefore if a cry goes forth come out of her my people then there has to be a church that God has prepare for such an undertaking by His Son Jesus in order for the people to go into; so they can be taught the truth and they accept that truth and meet the standard or criteria that God has planted or set forth, then they can qualify for an eternal existence. In Revelation 20: 5-8 but the rest of the dead lived not again until the thousand years were finished. This is the first resurrection. 6 Blessed and holy is he that hath part in the first resurrection: on such the second death hath no power, but they shall be priests of God and of Christ, and shall reign with him a thousand years. 7. And when the thousand years are expired Satan shall be loosed out of his prison. 8 and shall go out to deceive the nations which are in the four quarters of the earth, Gog and Magog to gather them together to battle the number of whom is as the sand of the sea.

This is when the last resurrection will take place which John spoke of in JOHN 11:19-24 and many of the Jews came to Martha and Mary, to comfort them concerning their brother Lazarus. 20 then Martha, as soon as she heard that Jesus was coming, went and met him; but Mary sat still in the house. 21 then said Martha unto Jesus, Lord if thou hast been here, mine brother had not died. 22 but I know that even now whatsoever thou wilt ask of God, God will give it thee. 23 Jesus saith unto her, thy brother shall rise again. 24 Martha saith unto him, I know that he shall rise again in the resurrection at the last day. This is the resurrection in the last day that Martha was talking about; which will take place in the eight day or end of the seven day. A type of it was in the Old Testament when every Jewish baby boy hath to be circumcised on the eighth day which was a type of the earth being cleansed on the eighth day; which is a thousand year day.

Then Revelation 22:13 and he shewed me a pure river of water of life clear as crystal, proceeding out of the throne of God and of the lamb. I thank God through His Son Jesus Christ for allowing me to serve him in the beauty of His holiness and I have been obedient to Christ; and have been a student in the Holy bible by applying 2 TIMOTHY 2:15 to my life, study to shew thyself approved unto

God, a workman that needeth not to be ashamed, rightly dividing the word of truth. I love the word of God and it has produced ripe fruit in my life and all my accomplishments in following the footsteps of Jesus and the bible said in 1PETER 2:21-25 for even here unto were ye called: because Christ also suffered for us, leaving us an example, that ye should follow his steps. 22 who did no sin; neither was guild found in his mouth. 23 who when he was reviled, reviled not again; when he suffered; he threaten not' but committed himself to him that judge righteously. 24 who his own self bare our sins in his own body on the tree, that we, being dead to sins should live unto righteousness, by whose stripes ye were healed. 25 For ye were as sheep going astray; but are now returned unto the Shepherd and Bishop of your souls. I started out on this journey in dedicating my life to the Lord Jesus by starting a ten day fast without eating or drinking or tasting anything. I was blessed to make it seven days without water and ten days without food so I started out on the way that led to finding favor in the sight of the Lord and when I went into work the next day after being filled with the Holy Spirit; when you consider I did this as a new born babe in Christ. Where did this knowledge come from? I started out like I had been serving God all my life. This knowledge could only come forth from the scripture in PROVERBS 22:6 train up a child in the way he should go, and when he is old, he will not depart from it. I was raised up in a Christian home in the Pentecostal faith and I was taught to say my blessings before, breakfast, lunch and dinner. I was raised up in a the Church of God in Christ as a little boy and my Mother Lizzie 'Mitchell' Hudson received the Baptism of the Holy Spirit there under Reverend Perry Robinson and she even had a section of our wall in our house taking out so they could have church services there.

I did not know this till Pastor William Lee at Saint Paul Robinson Memorial Church of God in Christ came to my Mother funeral at the Gospel Assembly Church which my Mother attended for over sixty years and told how she was a pioneer in their church and had giving her a plague; which said (PIONEER RECOGNITION) St. Paul / Robinson memorial, Church of God in Christ. Hereby present this certificate to (THE HUDSON FAMILY) for being truth spiritual warriors, unselfishly dedicating their life's to serving God and forging the path for future generations to follow. August 19, 2007. Elder William H Lee Pastor: St Paul / Robinson Memorial C.O.G.I.C. And she read the holy bible to us and taught us to say our prayers before we went to bed each night and those principles that I was taught stay with me all my life. I grew up being conscience of God. We lived at 432 South Charles Street on the East side of town and we attended Allen Street School till I was in the fourth grade. I never forgot those great services from both churches which had a great influence in my life even until now.

How the Saints worship and praise the Lord with singing, music and dancing in the Holy Spirit, I remember there was a coal stove in the middle of the church on Charles street, at that time we lived on a gravel road and a milk wagon pulled by a horse and the milk man would deliver our milk to our door and place the milk in a container by the front door. This was in the early 1950's when Pentecost was Pentecost like it said in JEREMIAH 6:16 Thus said the Lord, Stand ye in the ways and see and ask for the old paths, where is the good way and walk therein and ye shall find rest for your souls, But they said. We will not walk therein. The same things that make rivers crooked is the same things that make men and women crooked, and that is following the path of least resistance. I wanted to get saved and filled with the Holy Spirit; with the evidence of speaking in other tongues; which is speaking in a heavenly language; which give you the power to overcome sin and treat everyone like Christ. This was the era that I was raised up in.

A few years later a teenage Evangelist came to Lansing, under the guidance of his parents and two sisters, his name was David Walker and they called him little David Walker and they traveled the country running Revivals and they decided to build a church and the name was Gospel Tabernacle out West Main Street in Lansing, Michigan; after running Revivals at the Prudent Auditorium and that's when my Mother started going to his church and later my father came to visit and received the Baptism of the Holy Spirit with the evidence of speaking in a heavenly language and he became a believer in the Non-Denominational Pentecostal Faith and we continued to attend services there. They decided to go back into the Evangelist field; then other pastors was sent there and continued to have a voice in the Lansing area.

This Church was different than The Church of God in Christ that was predominant black, and Gospel Tabernacle Church which was all white and they were mostly Southerners and this was before the Civil Rights movement and my father Lacy Hudson and his sister Aunt Beatrice Clement and her two children Charles and Barbara attended our Church and also a friend Bessie Summerville and we were all from the Springhill and the town was Arkadelphia and Smithton and the town was Gurdon Arkansas area. This young teenager was brilliant with the scriptures and people started leaving their churches of all faiths and start coming to his church under his parent's supervision. He was taught by our founder Brother: William Sowders and his assistant Brother Tommy, with the knowledge they had of the Holy Bible in accepting nothing but truth and they would settle for nothing less and there can be no contradiction of the scriptures and it has to make sense and proven with other scriptures to confirm what they interpret was true.

I was about six or seven years old when we attended Gospel Tabernacle Church and all the young children were tarrying for the Holy Spirit with the evidence in ACTS 2: 4 and they were all filled with the Holy Spirit, and began to speak in other tongues (Languages) as the Spirit gave them utterance. ACTS 8: 14, 15, 16, 17. Now when the apostles which were at Jerusalem heard that Samaria had received the word of God, they sent unto them Peter and John. 15 who when they were come down, prayed for them, that they might receive the Holy Spirit. 16. (For as yet he was fallen upon none of them: only they were baptized in the name of the Lord Jesus) 17 then laid their hands on them and they received the Holy Spirit. Then in ACTS 10:44 – 48 while Peter yet spoke these words, the Holy Spirit fell on them which heard the word. 45 and they of the circumcision which believed were astonished, as many as came with Peter, because that on the Gentiles also was poured out the gift of the Holy Spirit. 46 for they heard them speak with tongues, and magnify God, Then answered Peter. 47 can any man forbid water, that these should not be baptized, which have received the Holy Spirit as well as we? 48 and he commanded them to be baptized in the name of the Lord, then prayed they him to tarry certain days.

In ACTS 19: 1-6 and it came to pass, that while Apollo's was at Corinth, Paul having passed through the upper coasts came to Ephesus, and finding certain disciples. 2 He said unto them, have you reccived the Holy Spirit since ye believed? And they said unto him. We have not so much as heard whether there is any Holy Spirit. 3. And he said unto them, unto what then was you baptized? And they said, unto John's baptism. 4 then said Paul, John verily baptized with the baptism of repentance, saying unto the people, they should believe on him which should come after him. 5 when they heard this, they were baptized in the name of the Lord Jesus. 6 and when Paul had laid his hands upon them, the Holy Spirit came on them, and they spoke with tongues (Languages) and prophesied. What was so amazing little children four and five years old at the altar speaking in a heavenly language with others, the women working at the altar with the young children instructing them to praise the Lord saying, keep saying Praise Him, Praise Him, Praise Him with their little hands raised toward heaven and all of a sudden they would be touched by God's Holy Spirit and they began to speak in a heavenly language with tears of joy rolling down their cheeks actually talking to the great God of Heaven and Earth.

I was so fascinated with those experiences that I received and witness my brother and sisters and cousins and all the children worshiping and praising the Lord of their salvation, and then the Holy Spirit would touch many of them at the altar tarrying for the Holy Spirit and many received that wonderful Gift into their life's just like they did in the former reign or New Testament Church two thousand years ago in Jerusalem. And ACTS 1:8 but ye shall receive power, after that the Holy Spirit is come upon you, and ye shall be witnesses unto me both in Jerusalem, and in all Judea and in Samaria, and unto the uttermost part of the earth. Then in ACTS 2: 38-39 Then Peter said unto them, repent and be baptized every one of you in the name of Jesus Christ, for the remission of sins, and ye shall receive the Gift of the Holy Spirit, for the promise is unto you, and to your children, and to all that are afar off, even as many as the Lord our God shall call. Therefore the door has been open to the gentiles as well as God chosen people the Jewish Nation.

Then in EPHESIANS 2: 11-13 wherefore remember, that ye being in time past Gentiles in the flesh, who are called uncircumcision by that which is called the Circumcision in the flesh made by hands. 12 that at that time ye were without Christ, being aliens from the commonwealth of Israel, and strangers from the covenants of promise having no hope and without God in the world. 13 but now in Christ Jesus ye who sometimes were far off are made nigh by the blood of Christ. The Gentiles was the people that was cut off from God at that time, now its saying the door of salvation has been open up to the Gentiles, so they can be fellow heirs to the covenant of promise as it is for the Jewish Nation.

I try so hard to receive the Holy Spirit like many of the other children, but it never happened; but those experiences never left my mind I have always been conscience of what I say and what I did and I never forgot to pray each night before I went to bed, and that continued with me when I was going to Grade School, Junior High School and High School, into adult hood. I remembered my arms and hands being so tired and my mouth would become so dry in saying, praise him, praise him, praise him, I wanted the Holy Spirit more than anything else in life. There is a scripture in PROVERBS 22:6 Train up a child in the way he should go and when he is old, he will not depart from it. The young men would be at the altar instructing me in what to say and to keep saying praise him, praise him, praise him. I truly believe I had a conversion experience at the altar, which is a change of heart, that Jesus Christ had forgiven me of my sins in a sense, because I was under my parents care until the age of capability, then I would have to be responsible for my own sins. This went on for days, weeks, months and years and that's why I am a Born Again Christian today in the Non-Denominational Pentecostal Faith.

We were taught in church to live like Jesus Christ lived and it was not an option but it was necessary and vital, who was our example and laid the foundation; for us to build on the rock and that rock was Christ. In MATTHEW 21: 42 Jesus said unto them. Did you never read in the scriptures, the stone which the builders rejected, the same is become the head of the corner, this is the Lord's doing and it is marvelous in our eyes? That Christ never responded in a negative way or act in a way that would bring a reproach on His father. In PROVERBS 8: 22-30. The Lord possessed me in the beginning of his way, before his works of old. 23 I was set up from everlasting, from the beginning or ever the earth was. 24 when there were no depths. I was brought forth, when there were no fountains abounding with water. 25 before the mountains were settled before the hills was I was brought forth. 26 as of yet he had not made the earth nor the fields nor the highest part of the dust of the world. 27 when he prepared the heavens. I was there when he set a compass upon the face of the depth. 28 when he established the clouds above, when he strengthened the fountain of the deep. 29 when he gave to the sea his decree, that the waters should not pass his commandment, when he appointed the foundations of the earth. 30 then I was by him as one brought up with him, and I was daily his delight, rejoicing always before him.

This is definite explaining about Jesus existence. And if we would conduct ourselves like Christ; then he would give us the Holy Spirit. And that's how I live my life as a little boy; because I wanted the Holy Spirit like the other children were receiving it. I never received the Holy Spirit; but all those days, weeks, months and years going to Gospel Tabernacle Church out West Main Street in Lansing, Michigan. I have always been aware of those experiences since I was a little boy and have continued with me until the present. The work that little, David Walker, the teenage Evangelist about seventeen years old, who started a work here in Lansing, that has continued today; but after a few years they went back into the Evangelist field and now he is with the Assembly of God Churches. Since we sold our church in Lansing, Michigan which was Gospel Assembly Church; but prior to that time there were other ministers that were sent here to pastor the church and had different names but the same section of the 'Body of Christ'.

I went to the Assembly of God church; called the Church with all the flags and now The International Outreach Church. I went there because I love to testified about the glory of God and what he was doing in my life and at that time I was going through a Civil Lawsuit against General Motors, which was Spiritual and the Lord Jesus led me all the way to victory; because I stood up against injustice when I was left with no choice; but to stand up for righteousness, which is written in my first book 'Boxer of the Year' Hudson VGM. I would testify about what I was going through with General Motors and how the Lord was blessing me; in answering my prayers, my parents objected to this; so I decided to let my father know that as long as I was going there I had to testify to the glory of God; for this is how I have always been blessed; after a few times of him saying I should not tell people my business, (I said to him, since he was there before I was I would leave and attend another church until the lawsuit was over).

We have three children, Eric Linn Hudson, Alaina Marie Hudson, and our youngest Steven Michael Hudson and we wanted them after going to a white Churches to have some African American friends, and all three has grown up to be responsible adults and all three have Bachelor's Degrees, Eric received his from Ferris State University, Alaina received hers from Atlanta Clark University, and Steven from Michigan State University. After the Lord blessed me with the lawsuit; I decided to go back to Gospel Assembly Church and my father had died at that time. I remember my Mother called me when my wife and I was visiting Atlanta, Georgia where our daughter decided to live there with her young son Billy Earl Young; after graduating from the University there. We were at the Monorail train station parking lot, when my Mother called me on my cell phone and said your Dad asked her when was I coming home. She said your father is not going to make it. I said I would come home and she said it was no need for me to come home. He knew about the prayers that I had answered and my dedicated to Christ and how The Holy Spirit comes upon me when I pray for people.

The Bishop decided to close our church in Lansing, Michigan in the year 2005; by that time I had started back attending Gospel Assembly Church prior to closing it; and some of the people moved to other of our Churches in different States and some are still having church services in their homes on Sunday in Charlotte, Michigan and we still had the same pastor who was with us when the church was sold. He moved back to Indianapolis, Indiana and he promised he would look after us; and Pastor: Richard Workman; came as long as it was feasible for him to come, then the women continue to have services there, and since they don't have a pastor I decided to continued witnessing at the prisons in Ionia, Michigan. The first was at Riverside Correctional Facility with O'Neil and May Carter, who was the pastor of the prison ministry and they both could really sing and the prisoner always request them to sing our God is an Awesome God who reigns from heaven above, with power and might our God is an awesome God. They attended River Terrance Church in East Lansing across from Michigan State University. The warden there was Adrian Libolt; who also was the Pastor wife and we rode together several times to the prison ministry and we had some nice conversations on the way to and from the prison ministry.

The youths were there until they reached twenty one years of age and then they would move them to an adult prison. They finally closed it down and moved the prisoners to a prison in Jackson, Michigan. I started witnessing at the jail in Charlotte Michigan. I prayed the Lord would open a way for me to go witnessing to another prison and the Lord open the door for me to go to Bellamy Creek Correctional Facility in Ionia with Pastor: Richard Rienstra and his wife Carol who played the piano, and now with Pastor: Andy Hanson at the same facility. The Chaplain there was Daniel Thompson. They were also from the Christian Reform Church; but in Grand Rapids, Michigan. Most of our Churches are in the Southern States and Ninety-Nine percent of them are white and about one percent are African Americans. They are taught the truth and it's for all Nationalities regardless of their background; because it's the closest to the teachings of Jesus and the Apostles and they would have to love truth over false doctrine or they will not stay; for they would feel it's too hard and too strict to be like those Saints in the New Testament Church; that Jesus and the Apostles planted.

They would not have a vision of a restore church; that's going to operate just like the Former Church two thousand years ago that operated for forty years; before the Apostles were killed and the truth they taught faded to the dark ages, till God called Martin Luther; the reformer in 1517 who broke away from the Catholic Church and started the Lutheran Church. He protested against that movement and the Protestant Churches came out of that movement. The word Catholic means universal and she is the mother of all her daughters; which the book of Revelations refers to them as harlots. In REVELATION 17:5-6 and upon her forehead was a name written; MYSTERY, BABYLON THE GREAT, THE MOTHER OF HARLOTS AND ABOMINATIONS OF THE EARTH. 6 and I saw the woman drunken with the blood of the Saints and with the blood of the martyrs of Jesus; and when I saw her, I wondered with great admiration.

We are a section of the 'Body of Christ' in other words all our churches work together as one without any outside influences and we are not on television or radio and we believe the latter church is going to duplicate the first century church for the first seven and a half years of the close of the Gentile age or supremacy. Then there will be a God Gifted Ministry on the earth once again, to give the people one last chance to accept the truth; before the bride of Christ is taking up to third Heaven where God and His beloved Son resides; with all the Angelic hosts and then there will be silence in heaven for a half an hour; which is seven and a half years; then the wrath of God will be pour out on this ungodly world. In REVELATION 8:1 and when he had opened the seventh seal; There was silence in heaven about the space of half an hour; there's twenty four hours in a day, and three hundred and sixty days in a year for perfected time, divide twenty four into three hundred and sixty days for a year and you get fifteen years; and that's how you get the two seven and a half years of time.

Our teaching of the doctrine of the bible is so different than other Pentecostal Churches. We believe we have to speak in a heavenly language to receive the Holy Spirit. We have to live a Holy life, and we are preparing our people for eternity on the new earth, when a number no man can count will live throughout the seedless and endless ages of eternity, here on the new earth. In REVELATION 7:9 after this I beheld, and lo, a great multitude, which no man could number, of all nations, and kindred's and people and tongues, stood before the throne, and before the Lamb; clothed with white robes, and palms in their hands. And in Psalms 78:69 and he built his sanctuary like high places; like the earth which he hath established forever. The earth according to this scripture will always be inhabited forever with God's people.

We also believe and teach like the scriptures said in EPHESIAN 2:8-9 For by grace are ye saved through faith; and that not of yourselves; it is the gift of God; 9 not of works, lest any man should boast. According to this scripture it's a gift of God; in being saved from our past sins; because there is no work involved for our initial or beginning phase of our salvation. We just ask the Lord Jesus to forgive us for our past sins and he cleanses us; so there is no work involved in that particular scripture; for our pass sins; but for our future sins, then we need to read in 1 JOHN 2:1 my little children, these things write I unto you that ye sin not. And if any man sin, we have an advocate with the father, Jesus Christ the righteous. And Apostle Paul in ROMANS 3:25 whom God hath set forth to be a propitiation through faith in his blood, to declare his righteousness for the remission of sins; that are past, through the forbearance of God. Therefore Apostle Paul is saying in this scripture; that being saved is only for our past sins; and our future sins we have to ask forgiveness; for every scripture has to be placed in the right sequence and order; so there will be no conflict or contradiction with the other scriptures.

Apostle Paul said in 2 TIMOTHY 2:15 study to shew thyself approved unto God a workman that needed not to be ashamed; rightly dividing the word of truth. The great Apostle Peter said in 2 PETER 3:16 as also in all his epistles, speaking in them of these thing; in which are some things hard to be understood, which they that are unlearned and unstable wrest; as they do also the other scriptures, unto their own destruction. The God of heaven and earth brought or sent me to a people; that love the Lord thy God with all their heart, soul, mind and body. Jesus taught in MATTHEW 22: 37 Jesus said unto him, thou shalt love the Lord thy God with all thy heart and with all they soul, and with all thy mind. This is how I have been taught for almost forty three years. And God never changes from his plan that he started with Adam and eve. The Father and Mother of all living human being's. And of all the species of the earth, only humans have been chosen to bring in the divine plan of God; for salvation.

And God started six thousand years ago; and time has been lost and all the dates are not exact; but God is right on time to restore the church one more time, prior to the bringing into an end the Gentile's era or age. There are so many great Prophecy's that are yet to be fulfilled and this really is a great time to be living in which could very well be the time; that God will manifest himself with the latter church; that will coincide with the former church during the time of the New testament Church. I have been preparing myself for such a time as this. I believe one of the greatest assets of my life has been witnessing to people in all walks of life where ever I am at and feel the leading of the Holy Spirit that I should give them a tract with my picture and testimony on it; with my boxing picture on the cover 'Boxer of the Year' which is an eye opener. I have been to Alcoholic Anonymous, and meetings at the City Rescue Mission, and The Highway Safety meetings. I have even stood outside of General Motors on Logan Street and Olds Avenue passing out my testimony in the winter season endeavoring to win souls to the kingdom of God. I also went to the Fisher Body (GM) plant on Verlinden and Michigan avenue across the street from Sexton High School, where I attended and Graduated there in the class of '1962' I was passing out my tracts to the workers. I also went the Union Hall at Local 652; for the annual Civil Rights program for the employees of Oldsmobile, General Motor Main Plant 1, passing out my testimony about my first book 'Boxer of the Year' Hudson VGM. I also stood outside of the old Lansing Civic Center, passing out my 'Boxer of the Year' tracts, with my testimony of how God through His beloved Son Jesus Christ; filled me with His Holy Spirit and deliver me from, drinking, drugs, gambling establishments, partying and all that is in the world.

And I have been walking in newness of life since 9/5/1972. This was also in the in the winter time and it was real cold and I stood out there about an hour, while the annual Lansing District Golden Gloves Championships were held; and I was the number one boxer in the 126 pound Featherweight class for several years; and won several Championships; prior to being drafted in the U.S. Army where I was in Special Services on the Third U.S. Army Boxing team, station at Fort McClellan, in Anniston; Alabama where I was the base Champion and qualified to go to the Third US Army Championship at Fort Campbell, Kentucky, home of the Screaming Eagles, 101st Airborne unit; where I was nominated for The All Army 'Boxing team '1967'.

I also was Lansing, Michigan first 'BLACK' "Boxer of the Year" and New Al VanNess 'Appreciation Trophy' and to make Sports Memories' from '1947 to 1966' Al VanNess who was a Boxer, Trainer, Coach and Boxing Promoter, told me personal; that they did not want to give you. Boxer of the Year'. He said he told them I should have won it every year which I had boxed, and that was in 1964, 1965 and 1966; three years. Then they selected me for the "Boxer of the Year' Trophy, and then Al VanNess also chose to give me his Trophy. The New Al VanNess 'Appreciation Trophy' and I made 'Sports Memories' by out boxing two State Golden Gloves Boxing Champions and one was unbeaten with eight fights and seven Knockouts and TKO's and his last five did not go the distance. Here's how the article was written by Jim Wallington 'Sports Writer' Lansing State Journal '1966'. Elmo Hudson, three- times district Golden Gloves Champion; was named winner of the 'Boxer of the Year' Trophy, despite his lost in The State Finals; it was disclosed Elmo was boxing with three broken ribs. And Jim followed me throughout my boxing career with many great pictures and write-ups.

Then it was impressed on my mind to go to the prisons where I had been before; when I was boxing for Dick Letts of Lincoln Center on the Westside of Town; when I made 'Sports Memories' by out boxing two District and State Golden Gloves 'Boxing Champions. The 'Sports Writer' wrote; each of the boy's trainers tabs his boxer as the probable winner. Each has an equal chance to win but this writer bends toward Stemler; for two reasons. First, all he has needs to land is one punch. He can spend the entire fight looking for the opening for the one blow and when he finds it, brother, look out.

In eight Golden Gloves bouts in two years, he's won seven by Knockouts or TKO's and only one by decision. None of his victories last year ever went the distance—three in the districts and two in the State meet. Few Golden Glovers can match that record. In both of his State bouts he was being battered and trailed in points before exploding the knockout punches. So you can see why match maker Al VanNess finds special delight with this weight division, but he hesitates in naming a favorite. It's hard to pick against a champion and in this case there are three of them. I could not have accomplished what I have in life as a Born Again Christian, with the evidence of speaking in a heavenly language, like the Apostles and Saints received it; in the New Testament Church; without my boxing experiences in the life; I lived before becoming a Christian and has become such a great part of my life; in every opportunity I see to witness; I take advantage of it; and seize upon the moment to tell them about my testimony and that is one of the main reason I have been so blessed.

I brought an advertising kit, with business cards and book marks; with the information about my book on them. I love witnesses to the saved and unsaved; since I became a Christian on September 5, 1972 the first day on my job; after receiving the Holy Spirit the night before; in the engine plant at The 'Oldsmobile', General Motors main plant 1. I went to my job in the test room, testing engine for defects by push button machines. I was witnessing to every employee who worked in there that I had received the Holy Spirit and one man made the statement; that won't last long, and I had an Aunt that said that won't last two weeks. It's been almost forty three years and I am still in love with the only love letter from heaven from God himself. I felt everybody would want to hear, how I had been Saved and Filled with God's Holy Spirit; with the evidence of speaking in a heavenly language. As it is written in the book of ACTS 2:4 and they were all filled with the Holy Spirit; and began to speak with other tongues 'languages' as the Spirit gave them utterance. This gave me the power to accomplish; whatever the Holy Spirit was prompting me to do, and I have been able to follow the leading of the Spirit as it said in ROMAN 8:14 for as many; as are led; by the Spirit of God, they are the sons of God.

Then in ROMAN 8:16 the Spirit itself beareth witness with our Spirit, that we are the children of God. And then in 1 JOHN 3:22 and whatsoever we ask, we receive of him; because we keep his commandments, and do those things that are pleasing in his sight. Those three scriptures go together which tells why the Spirit of God has confirmed his word. This let us know that God has heard our prayer; because of the life I have lived for Jesus Christ and the God Gifted Ministry, who taught us; as it said in 2 PETER 2: 20-21 knowing this first; that no prophecy of the scripture is of any private interpretation. 21 for the prophecy came not in old time by the will of man, but holy men of God spoke as they were moved by the Holy Spirit. Then when I ask him according to his will; then I am blessed by him according to his pure unadulterated truth of the word of God.

That's why the Spirit beareth witness with our Spirit; that we are the children of God. And the way it bears witness with me is not only the results; that I received after I touch God and it doesn't have to happen when I pray deeply in the morning or afternoon; but also in our churches or driving my car and wherever I may be in a spiritual setting. And it took a lot of work by applying the word of God to my life to the fullness, and I have never been influence or persuaded in what others are doing. I am influence and persuaded in the knowledge the Lord has imparted to me by having some of the best Holy Spirit Filled teaching, and I have planted those truths in my spiritual heart; 'which is the mind' so deeply that most people that have heard me speak and quote the scriptures wonder where did I get this knowledge from? And of course it came by the Bishop and the Ministry in our section of the 'Body of Christ' has produced those ingredients and results into my life.

When the pure unadulterated word of God touches the Holy Spirit in my life; when I am praying with conviction; the Holy Spirit moves me; and that's how I know God heard me through his beloved son Jesus Christ; in what I have been praying for. Many times I pray in conversing with the Lord and even then because of my dedication he touches me in just showing his appreciation in the sincerity of my reaction to his word; as a result of applying it to my life. 1 TIMOTHY 2:5 for there is one God and one mediator between God and man, the man Christ Jesus. So Jesus takes our prayers or petition before God the father for us; and I know through personal experience; for me it has taking me almost forty three years as a Born Again Christian in The Non – Denominational Pentecostal Gospel Assembly Churches; to reach the place; that I am; in things that pertain to life and godliness. 2 PETER 1:3 according as his divine power hath given unto us all thing's that pertain unto life and godliness through the knowledge of him that has called us to glory and virtue.

I have also been taught by our Ministry; that we cannot go any farther in God than the knowledge we have of him. It is really no different than in Natural life; as it is in the Spiritual life; for if we apply the word of God to our life, by allowing it to assimilate, digest and become part of us, then we will grow, prosper, mature and develop in portraying our life in Christ Jesus. And by the same token if we fail to apply these truths to our life, we would become as a sounding brass or a tingling cymbal. In 1 CORINTHIANS 13:1 though I speak with the tongues of men and of angels, and have not charity, I am become as sounding brass or a tingling cymbal, our life would then be displeasing to our Lord. I have been taught the word of God with such conviction; that I always want to respond to any person in a positive way in order for my life to be pleasing in His sight. The experiences have had plays an important part in my life by those truths that has been deposit into my mind has continue to position myself to receive from the Lord. I have continued to build on that solid foundation; which is Christ Jesus my Lord; and I know through my experiences according to the word of God; in seeking truth with no contradiction of the other scriptures has enabled me to rise above this earthly way of thinking and doing things in a Spiritual manner. I believe the Spirit of the living God; prepare me for such a time as this in using the experiences that I went through with General Motors for seventeen long years from August 19, 1983 to July of 2000. Here's some of the teaching that prepare me for that seventeen year Civil Rights lawsuit; against the great General Motors.

On September 28, 1980, my pastor Fred Young, during one of his teaching sessions, let us know that time was running out; everyone that has tried it has failed. We cannot do it in our own strength. Paul depicted it best in the six and seven of ROMANS 6:20, He was letting us know about sinners; for he said, when we were the servants of sin, we were free from righteousness. This is a peculiar setting; but just turn it around and phrase it this way; for when we were the servant of righteousness we were free from sin. We can make sin our servant or we can be a servant to sin. We cannot do evil or be possessed with the devil when we are full of the Spirit. We cannot be taking over by the Devil or Satan. This is when we are free from sin. When we are doing right, like it said in 1 JOHN 3:7 little children, let no man deceive you; he that doeth righteousness is righteous, even as he is righteous. We cannot sin when his seed remain in us.

Therefore we cannot sin when we are putting the word of God into practice in our life's; anytime you are doing God's work and being obedient to his word, you cannot sin, that makes sense; so when we began to see what Apostle Paul was saying. See there is a condition existing in me; when I would do good evil is present in me. The good I would do I do not, the evil I would not do, that I do; therefore it is no more I that doeth it; but sin that dwelleth in me. He said I know in my flesh dwelleth no good thing. So when on living after the flesh; when the flesh is influencing my life; then I sin, I do evil, because there is no good in that flesh, it's a fallen condition, therefore there is another law working in my members; it's the law of sin and death. It is not the law of righteousness; it is not the law of life. It's the law of sin and death.

It is that sinful nature wanting to do those things that is contrary to God. Now when I do that I would not do; it is no more I that is doing it; but it is that other nature; that flesh life that's causing me to do what I am doing. So we see it cannot be done to rend ourselves of sin in our own strength or ingenuity. It is a feat that has never been accomplished or ever will be accomplished, except with the aid and assistant of the word of God. It takes the Spirit of God to get the job done. Paul looked at himself. He just paraded himself out before himself. Do we dare to parade ourselves out before ourselves; to see what kind of individual we are in, that is exactly what Apostle Paul was doing. When he did he said oh wretched man that I am; look what a state I am in, who shall deliver me from the body of this death. I thank God; if the works that is prevailing in me and my life goes on and prevail. I am going down in death; there is no hope of life through Jesus Christ our Lord.

That is the only way there is no other provision, there is no other way, human being have ever risen above the condition of their flesh; if that is the case, the secret is learning the word of God. Do what the bible tells us to do, be the kind of individual God tells us to do. Somebody might say; how are we going to do this, to be free from sin; let's make a fair comparison, when we get ready to do something, or think something, to say something, see if it is allowed in the word of God; see if God permit us to do that, We do not have to look any farther than the word of God; for a guide line. Apostle Paul even pointed out to us and made us aware that we are not allowed to judge another man servant, to his own master he stand or falls, according to the rules and regulation of his own master. Therefore who are thou old man; that judgest another man servant, then when we passed judgment or looking at a condition or something fail to meet our approval we must consider doe's it meet with God's approval, and how does God feel about it, how does God look at it. We must judge according to the word of God. If we judge any other way we are judging another man servant.

We do not have that right; it is unlawful for us to do it. He either stands or falls to his own master. But when we example that individual by the word of God; it is not us that's judging, but the word of God. It is his word that is judging you and judging that condition to see whether or not it is justified in his sight and how he feels about it. When we judge a thing by the word of God, it is not us that judging; but the word of God. It's his word that is judging you and judging that condition to see whether or not it is justified in his sight and how he feels about it; we are not entitled to our own opinion; the bible must have the final word. So our hope is in him, there is no other direction we can go. And when we look at our life and the time we have left, what else can we do; but buried our head in the word of God and meditate on the things of God.

What else can we do but pray and seek God to stay filled with his Spirit if we are to survive. There is no other way out or remedy or solution to our problem or anybody or condition; but to follow that procedure and prepare ourselves for the work of God. If we don't do it that way; we are sure to qualify as a vessel of dishonor as anything. If we would understand when God judges a condition he does not always judge it the same way, just like it was in the days of those Apostles, with Ananias and Sapphira. Do you think they were the only two; that lied to those Apostles; do you think they could dealt with the thousands and thousands of people and only two of them told them a lie. We have a record those two die.

It shows God was confirming his word with signs and wonders. Often we have a longing for a restore church, what we expect to see, the dead raised to life again, the blind see, the lame walk. Did you know in that kind of church people fall over dead, they die simply for telling a lie, are you aware of that? Have you ever consider or analyze that or giving any thought to that. If we were in a restore church right now and some of the things we are doing we could die for it. How many ever put that as a part of a restore church, alright that's a part of it. I was going to point out; just like Ananias and Sapphira fell over dead for telling a lie to Apostle Peter; for what they sold a piece of property for. That was just as much as God confirming their word with signs following as it was in raising the dead, or opening the blinded eyes or cause the lame to walk.

The point is God did not cause everyone to die who lie to those God gifted Apostles. He went on and let others ridicule and scorn and persecute and serve as a thorn in the flesh of those Apostles. He let them go on and did not do anything about it or let them go on for years for any action was taking at all. He allowed that to use them as a vessel of dishonor that they might help to perfect the saints in the church. We have to recognize the cross we are to take up and follow Christ daily exist in the church; it is not outside mixing with the world of man-kind. Somebody might say, I really have to take up my cross on the job or I will go under, you are not taking up your cross there, you are choosing that job and can leave. You don't have to stay there if condition is not suitable, you can quit; you take that by choice; but what about in God's church?

We cannot be saved and leave, so we stay. Here's where we take up our cross, here's where we are faced with those conditions; that goes cross grain to you and conflict with our ideas and feelings things don't harmonize with you, it's in the church; so here's where we take up our cross daily and follow the Lord. A vessel of honor and a vessel of dishonor can be in church for the express purpose of perfecting that vessel of honor to go on in God, till he's perfected. Then the Lord will dealt with the vessel of dishonor and they can be in church; for the purpose of perfecting that vessel of honor to go on in God, till he's perfected. Then the Lord will dealt with the vessel of dishonor and take it out of existence and annihilates it. We have to look at it; for thing's happens to us in the church is for a reason; it's not accidental, it's a purpose, a motive, a reason. We should see what kind of message God is endeavoring to convey to us over here in his kingdom when we began to analyze that, and example it like that, scrutinize it very closely, and bring it under that big powerful microscope until we can see this over here in the church.

We are to take nothing for granted or pan it off too lightly; even though a person is a vessel of dishonor. Paul said if any man will purge himself from these he can be a vessel of honor, fit for the master use, so then whatever happens to us if we would example it and look for God in it and see what is transpiring in our life's and what's taking place, knowing that when we are over in the kingdom of God and born into his kingdom; that somewhere their whatever happens God is endeavoring to use that to take us on to perfection. He's trying to perfect our life. He's using that to show us our weaknesses and flaws and short coming in our life's so we can do something about it. That's his purpose and his motive, that's his purpose, that's his way of working.

He have to let sin condition to exist; for us to see that God will do it. He will allow that to go on and be present in our midst and allow pressure and persecution to come against us from within the church in order for us to see ourselves; that we might do something about it and be saved and not go down in defeat and be lost, by starting off as a vessel of honor and ending up as a vessel of dishonor, that's just throw out with the trash and refuse. And so here we are over in God's kingdom endeavoring to be saved; wanting our lives to measure up wanting to be free of sin and the way to be free of sin is to do right. There's no other way but to do right. The only time we are free of righteousness is when sin is operating. So we want to be free of sin, we have been free of righteousness.

We have been taking over by sin we have lived where we were not righteous. We want to live right and be free of sin and just resolve that condition that Paul was describing in (ROMAN 6:20) when it dawn on Paul, what the law of Moses served. In the Law of Moses, sin could be present, sin could exist, but he said without the law sin was dead; it was dead; because I did not understand it. I did not know what sin was; but when the law came sin revived and I died. I died because I was made aware or conscience what sin was, and I found myself in a condition that I could not get the victory over sin; therefore it was made appear that the law was sinful; but when I begin to analyze it. I could see the law was good. The law was not sinful, it was good. It was good because it pointed out sin and made me aware of sin. It made sin exceedingly sinful and therefore it was a condition in me and I could see the law was good; and it is not sinful at all. It brought death; because it made us aware of sin and know what sin was.

Paul said I would not have known what sin was except the law said, thou shall not lust, you are not to lust. I would not have known what it was about. I would not have been able to categorize it or put a title on it. I could not isolate it in my life except the law made a statement on these lines and declare certain things to be sin. I would not have been able to do it. So God's law is what points up sin in our life and makes us aware and conscience of sin. So it's putting into practice that law which will eventually free us from sin; by being obedient to the law of God. I don't have reference to the Law of Moses. I have reference to the law of God, by putting into practice the law of God will free us of sin by making us aware of what sin is.

And if we don't obey that law, it brings death to us. The knowledge of that law does not bring death; but life and enable us to live and not die. So look what God has called us to look at the opportunity God is setting out before us. He's enabling us not to be in darkness. Often Paul would say you are not in darkness; ignorant state of mind. We know the devil cannot possess us or use us when we are obedient of the law of God.

When the Spirit of God is active in our life, there has to be sin, there has to be something that cause us to deviate from the law of God. The law of God, the Spirit of God, to give the devil a foothold or place in our life it has to be a putting down of the law and standard of God for him to get in and operate and work. A vessel of dishonor can cause us to be a instrument in his hand. Sometime we are obsessed of the devil; that is we are pre-occupied and he places feelings and ideas on us; but that's different from being possess of the devil. This is an altogether different function and work. We can be preoccupied with certain thoughts and feelings hit us; and causes us to lean on certain thoughts and actions; it can influence us alone that line; yet not being taking over by the devil, where he possesses us or influence us or control us, that's what happens when you are devil possess, he influence us. He controls and directs us that way.

When we are preoccupied with a thought we can cast that aside; it be not strong enough to control us to cause us to be seize or overpower us. The law of God allows us to see that. We can see that through the word of God, so God is interest in us. He's hot leaving us in darkness or a state of ignorance. He's not leaving us in a condition where we don't understand and don't know or familiar or acquainted with the working of God; and the law and order of God. The language of God we are familiar with those things; there are people that don't understand the word of God. We know the time periods in the bible are used differently. We can look at the word of God and read it and arrived at an understanding of what God means when he said certain things. I believe it's in the second chapter of Genesis. There he uses the word day it refers to a thousand years. Then in HEBREWS 3:15 a day meaning a period of forty years, termed it and used it that way; so we look at the text, what is the text, what is it saying; then we get the context and see what surrounds that text, when we do we can read the word of God and derive the meaning out of it.

In GENESIS 2: 1-25; he's talking about a period of two thousand years. The scripture; then in HEBREW 3:15 that period of time where he suffer there manner in the wilderness was a forty year span of time. Again in 2 Peter 3:8 But beloved, be not ignorant of this one thing, that one day is with the Lord as a thousand years, and a thousand years as one day. He's using time that way, and refers to a day like that. The same rule applies to other scriptures. We look at the text, then the context and see how it's used and how it is applied and knowing how to put the proper interpretation on the word of God. And others have failed to see that when they see a day to them; it means the same period of time. They say how do we know? A perfected day is three hundred and sixty days. We understand the bible. Peter with his knowledge he wrote concerning Paul. In 2 PETER 3: 16 as also in all his epistles, speaking in them of these things; in which are some things hard to be understood, which they that are unlearned and unstable wrest, as they do also the other scriptures, unto their own destruction.

You cannot reach out and receive it with a carnal mind. Some people think you can; but that's far from the truth, they cannot do it. God did not design it that way. They feel like they love the Lord and been converted they should be able to set down and read the bible and get the same understanding as anybody else, and have the same interpretation of the word of God, that is not true, that's why Peter said our beloved brother Paul wrote some things hard to be understood that they which are ignorant and unlearned wrest the scriptures to their own destruction. They are not tutor in the things of God and don't know how to apply it. The word of God and make a mess out of it; but here God is opening up our understanding and doing it right because God is dealing with our lives. He has an interest in our life.

He's endeavoring to perfect our life; when Jesus went into the wilderness. He had not come from a strong anointing or was perfect. He was weak, when Satan challenged him. It could have been easy under other conditions or circumstances to reject Satan. He was talking to a hungry man; but Jesus had God word in his life. He would say it is written in MATTHEW 4:1-4 then was Jesus led up of the spirit into the wilderness to be tempted of the devil. 2 and when he had fasted forty days and forty nights, he was afterward hungered. 3 And when the tempter came to him, he said, if thou be the son of God, command that these stones be made bread. 4 but he answered and said, it is written, Man shall not live by bread alone, but by every word that proceedeth out of the mouth of God.

It would be easy for us, to go on to perfection; if the Spirit of God was strong. But God does not work that way. It has to be a spearhead, someone has to be the example and be in the forefront. They are tempted on every hand. It will be someone who went through it, that's why it was said about Jesus in HEBREW 4:14-15 seeing then that we have a great high priest, that is passed into the heavens; Jesus the Son of God; let us hold fast our profession. 15 for we have not a high priest which cannot be touched with the feeling of our infirmities; but was in all points tempted like as we are, yet without sin. He had already went through it and tested and tried on every hand. He had been tried when he was hungry to see if he would exercise the power God had delegated to him; for his own purpose or personal use. He passed every test. God will try us also. He will have a people to serve as an example out here. When a person come to us with a problem we can say, we have been through it and know what you are going through, and here's how we came out of it. We resorted to the word of God. We located ourselves in the word of God and to know God was dealing in our life. He was working with us to take us to perfection and here's how we overcame it. We looked to God in prayer. We fell on our knees and cried, fasted and the God of heaven finally came to our rescue. He saw we were determined to do the right thing; that we would not succumb to evil even at the peril of our life.

We were determined that Satan would not influence us, now it will work for you. Where is God going to find that element of people; most people are pamper with a sugar cover message. We want a church that's free from sin 1 PETER 4:1 forasmuch then as Christ hath suffered for us in the flesh; arm yourselves with the same mind:

for he that hath suffered in the flesh hath ceased form sin, we are depriving ourselves from the things we want and long for and our nature craves and wants and long for and thirst after and in quest of, we are depriving ourselves from it we are holding it right there and saying, God there are things that are more important with us than to sin raveling in the flesh; by catering to that kind of life. We want that which instill such qualities in a man like Paul from persecuting the church to one sitting over in a prison house, and he was not grumbling or complaining or saying the sacrifice is too hard.

He could have been married and have a wife to lead around like his brethren Peter and was allowed to be married. He was not complaining. He sat in a cold wet dungeon and he started to sing and glorified the God of heaven, that God might manifest his approval on his life; God cause the jail to quiver and shake and the bonds fell off their hand, and shackles from their feet and set them free. That God might be glorified as a result of the life they were living. God is endeavoring to work through us. It will cost us something. Paul said in PHILIPPIANS 3:14 I pressed toward the mark for the prize of the high calling of God in Christ Jesus. That's what we are pressing for, we are endeavoring to glorified him to pull off our mortal bodies and put on our immortal bodies; a new glorified body. We are trying to reach that state where we are not confined to this earth, where we can travel out to third heaven where God and the angels are.

In order to qualify for that kind of existence, it will cost us something, sin is not worth it. God is giving us experiences. God said a righteous man can fall seven times and God will raise him up. Look at David he was just as guilty of murder as if he put the sword through Uriah himself. He also committed adultery; but God forgave David; because the bible said David follow God all the days of his life. David had weaknesses, but he did not deviate from God. He never put anything any greater than God. That's why God loved him. Paul said in 1 CORINTHIANS 11:29-30. For he that eateth and drinketh unworthily, eateth and drinketh damnation to himself, not discerning the Lord's body. 30 for this cause many are sickly and weakly among you, and many sleep (died). When we make a mistake God will raise us up. Look at the percentage of ever getting in the

Body of Christ. God so cared for us and opened our understanding to the truth of the word of God. Let's not get upset and condemn the Body of Christ. God could cut us off forever. Business will pick up after a while; for the people of God; so let's stay faithful.

Jesus said in JOHN 17: 12 While I was with them in the world, I kept them in thy name: those that thou gravest me, I have kept, and none of them is lost, but the son of perdition, that the scripture might be fulfilled. Also in ACTS 2:47 praising God, and having favour with all the people. And the Lord added to the church daily such as should be saved. It is up to God, we might influence them, but it's God that add sheep to the flock. God sheep hear his voice another they will not follow. Paul had to warn them concerning preachers coming in sheep clothing, but inwardly they are ravening wolves. Our present shows we are interested. Alright Brother Dick will you take up the offering, God is concern for us. He knows our needs; Oh heavenly Father, thank you; for the privilege of coming before you; once again. Our confidence is in you and the concern you have for your people, all the spoken and unspoken requests. Oh God go with us and keep us by thy Spirit, we will give you the honor and the glory, thou so deserve, you know we were caught up in the quire mire of sin and death, and you had mercy on us and came to our rescue. Thank you heavenly Father; can we give him a praise, praise God, praise God; praise His wonderful Holy name.

Here's what our leaders taught us at our Church Convention in Louisville, Kentucky. He starts off repeating is the essence of learning, essential is the important part. In the book of EZEKIEL 47:1-5 afterward he brought me again unto the door of the house; and behold, waters issued out from under the threshold of the house eastward: for the forefront of the house stool toward the east, and the waters came down from under from the right side of the house, at the south side of the altar. 2 then he brought me out of the way of the gate northward, and led me about the way without unto the utter gate by the way that looketh eastward; and behold, there ran out waters on the right side. 3 and when the man that had the line in his hand went forth eastward, he measured a thousand cubits, and he brought me through the waters; the waters were to the angles. 4

again he measured a thousand, and brought me through the waters; the waters were to the knees. Again he measured a thousand, and brought me through, the waters were to the loins. 5 afterward he measured a thousand; and it was a river that I could not pass over; for the waters were raised, waters to swim in, a river that could not be passed over.

A cubit in the old Testament was eighteen inches (now it's fifteen inches) If it said feet; it still would be the same; because in the bible it is always a year. It's really a measure like a twelve feet ruler. In the book of REVELATION 11:1 and there was given me a reed like unto a rod, and the angel stood, saying, rise, and measure the temple of God, and the altar and them that worship therein. This is a perfect hookup. It starts in the book of EXODUS 25: then the next fifteen chapters to the fortieth chapter gives the size and measurement and description of everything that went into the church house in Israel. An altar symbolizes where the beast was offered or there was a square thing like our bible stand with iron grapes on it with an ash pan underneath it. That is where they laid the animal and offered it for a sacrifice. The church house in the Old Testament was called the slaughterhouse. And it still is. It slaughter the old man; that old sinful nature in us. If you want to be educated in the bible you should read this. All this is a type, and The Apostle Paul touched on this in the book of HEBREWS 9: the book of HEBREWS was written to the Hebrew Christians; never-the-less; we have become a Spiritual Jew.

We can convert that over when we read it and get great and valuable lessons. We must learn to transpose the word of God. The Old Testament is the New Testament contain. The New Testament is the Old Testament explained. The New Testament is contained in the Old Testament. From MALACHI back to GENESIS the Jews read it and never did see the New Covenant in it at all. Jesus told them in JOHN 5:39 search the scriptures; for in them ye think ye have eternal life: and they are they who testify of me. All they had was the Old Testament; but that was enough; eternal life was in there which pertain to an eternal existence. Jesus looked at them and said; ye will not come to me to fulfill the scriptures and bring it out to you, so you can have everlasting life.

In the book of LUKE 24:32 then open he there understanding; that they might believe the scriptures. Jesus was the key man, a teacher and he could open up the scriptures. All the types and shadows pictures he opened up to them. Then he told them all the lawyers, a lawyer was a very efficient bible teacher. Nicodemus was a lawyer. He was a great teacher in Israel. Every time you run across the word scribes in the bible; it means a teacher of the law. They interpret the word of God. They were well versed in the scriptures of the bible. They interpret the law to the people. Jesus said every scribe that is instructed in the New Covenant was in the kingdom of heaven. The kingdom of heaven; was the church at that time. And it was the New Covenant under Christ. He said, all ye scribes or lawyers, that will come to me and listen to what I have to say and explain the New Covenant from the Old Covenant.

Then you will be like a householder in MATTHEW 13: 52 then said he unto them; therefore every scribe, who is instructed unto the kingdom of heaven is like unto a man that is a householder, which bringeth forth out of his treasure things new and old. The temple had a huge treasure house in it. You can read it in the book of Kings and in Isaiah; where the servants of the men of Babylon, where the Spy's came over from Babylon, when Hezekiah was the King in Israel; these Spy's came over and Hezekiah received them graciously, and did not have very much discernment. He did not know what they were up to; and he showed them; all around the palace grounds, similar to when Khrushchev came over here to America and the government spent a million dollar on him. He was already responsible for thirty million people in the Ukraine under Stalin. He was their right hand man. Our government spent a million dollar on him, flying him all over the United States. In EZEKIEL 16: it speaks of valuable materials. In little Palestine, Hezekiah was the King and David had preceded him in gathering all kinds of souvenirs and fine gold and art work and gifts of every kind. This was the treasure house.

David was the only man to conquer Damascus in all the Kings of Israel. Those Spy's came in and King Hezekiah show them his treasures, Isaiah came in afterwards, and asked him what did these men want and he said to congratulate him on his recovery from a very painful skin disease; when he was set to die and the Prophet Isaiah told him he would not die, but to take a piece of fig and lay it on the sore and you will be healed and live and not die. He told them this is what David and his son Solomon brought in and show them all his treasures; so Isaiah rebuked him for that and foretold the later captivity of Judah by Babylonia. Isaiah told him they will be back and strip you of all your treasures; In the meantime Sargon quickly defeated Merodach and recaptured Babylon. Isaiah was the main brain thrust; the Kings right hand man, he had been the counselor to four different Kings. A few years later they came back to Babylon and stripped Israel of everything with the temple gold and the outstanding people. The prophet Isaiah was about a hundred years old when he died. In 1 CORINTHIANS 10:11 now all these things happened unto them for examples; and they were written for our admonition, upon whom the ends of the world are come.

Those examples were pictures of the New Testament in dark sayings of types and shadows, telling about an event that had happened or transpire in reality; for instance the New Testament is the Old Testament explained and the Old Testament is the New Testament contained. Israel was uninformed, they would not pray and ask God for knowledge to learn the New Testament scriptures. When Jesus came they did not understand what he was talking about; imagine fifteen hundred lambs was offered for fifteen hundred years, letting them know; a person would be killed and shed his life blood; and that blood would serve or atone for the sins of the nations. When John the Baptist saw Jesus; he said; behold here comes the Lamb of God. He could have said; and you are going to kill him. You are going to crucify him and nail him to a cross.

His blood is so precious in God sight that he will be the salvation of Israel. If we are not careful we will crucify Christ Spiritually. You will be a Judas in the Body of Christ. Isaiah said the report will only vex their spirit when they hear it. Christ was a reporter. The God Gifted Apostles were reporters. They would report these happenings to Israel then they would turn against them. It would just vex them or stir their spirit. If we are not careful we will get mad at the word of God. ISAIAH the fifty-third chapter and PSALMS the second chapter, both were talking about Christ and his death; the most outstanding things Christ did was recorded in these two chapters. The Jews read those verses over and over and took no interest in it. They would not pray about the meaning or interpretation of those scriptures. They did not care what those scriptures were conveying; they trusted their own fate and understanding of those scriptures. The Jews said; we have no King but Caesar; he's our King. They knew that Rome had slain their millions around the world. They knew they had burn cities down, and they knew Caesar was a whole dynasty of lying Romans, that had inhabit the earth and slaughter by the millions and burn their cities all over the world. Yet they said we have no King; but Caesar.

He told them about themselves, and they could not comprehend his words; for they were dull of hearing. Some people have said I just love PSALMS 23, the Lord is my Shepherd, I shall not want, I get so much comfort out of those scriptures. How much comfort do we get out of the scriptures that said, you will be judge for every idle word spoken; that goes cross grain to the word of God? Jesus said in JOHN 6:53, then Jesus said unto them, verily, verily, I say unto you, except you eat the flesh of the son of man and drink his blood, you have no life in you. The Old and New Testament is interwoven together, the person that is interested have to be vital concern with their life to fine those precious saying in the Old Testament. Apostle Paul said to Titus, God promise life to his son before the world begun. The Jews knew from PSALMS 22: 1-31 that they would pierce his hand and feet. They did not see the Lamb being sacrifice on the altar. Our leader did not want his churches to be left in the dark. He wants us to be well versed and informed in the words of God and His beloved son Jesus Christ.

When we read certain passages and don't understand what message it is trying to convey to us; a symbol is a natural object that portray a Spiritual truth. The Lord wanted a lamb when it was a year old. It is one of the cleanest animals in the world. God wanted a lamb when it was young and full of life; and did not have any battle scars, or blemishes or disease. The Lord said he wanted it while it was young and tender. He wanted it, before it got scratches or bitten by another animal. He did not want any blemish on it, when it was offered for a sin offering. The reason it was showing His son, who was to be offered up for the sins of the whole world, and how clean God wants us to be; when we are forgiven for our sins. We were like a young tender lamb without a blemish on it, and that is what happens when we are born of the Holy Spirit, which is called a new birth. God is a conservative God. In ECCLESIASTES 12:13-14 let us hear the conclusion of the whole matter, fear God, and keep his commandments; for this is the whole duty of man 14 for God will bring every work into judgment; with every secret thing, whether it is good or whether it is evil.

DELIGATED AUTHORITY

The preacher who surveyed his congregation, just prior to his message, lost his will to cry out against sin and evil. He lost his courage because his eyes fell upon Mr. Important, Miss Society Lady, and Mr. Sportsman. He may have seen in his congregation, some of the same members that were seen in - —Pilgrim progress. The fear of being unpopular and offending the attendees, especially the board of deacons, have ruined many a preachers. His message wilts, loses its meaning. "You are all sinners, more or less. If you don't repent, to a certain extent, and be converted, in a measure, you will be doomed, to a degree and you may perish. Pulpits and religious institutions are saturated with men and women; that are trained speakers. They are clever, talented, artistic, creative, skilled, and appealing, buy their pointless in the substance of their message. We are inundated with sputtering speakers, podium pounders, pulpit pumpers and flamboyant flag wavers; but few who stand tall for holiness, purity, God and the bible truth.

It is right to fear offending people, but if teaching the truth is an offense; then shut your eyes and pull the trigger; else you are following the crowd and not a leader. Samuel said this to Saul: 1 SAMUEL 13:13-14 and Samuel said to Saul; thou hast done foolishly, thou hast not kept the commandment of the Lord thy God; which he commanded thee; for now would the Lord establish thy kingdom upon Israel forever. 14 but now thy kingdom shall not continue. "It took courage to tell a king that he has done foolishly. Samuel loved God and he loved Saul. He believed in God and righteousness and was willing to make any sacrifice and do what was right and best for God's people to who he was sent. He sounded the cry; his trumpet did not give an uncertain sound. Just compare Jesus disciples to today's men of cloth.

They were poor, uneducated, uncomplicated, none assuming, and without silver and gold. Today's group are well paid, well educated, politically popular, sought after as entertainment speakers, live in the best of houses, and dine at the finest of restaurants. Perhaps this comparison is meaningless, we accept that assumption, but the strength of today's message is flat, flabby and meaningless compared to the message that those early church disciples preached. They stirred both heaven and hell. They saved some, and doomed others, and made the whole world guilty before God. What is contemporary Philosophy compared to the message Jesus taught in MATTHEW 5-7? Jesus gave to Israel and the world what was a message that reflects a pagan culture; the sinners will not be convicted of his sins. The church will become a social function and the souls of many will not be able to see the gates of glory.

The message must be simple but sure, it must be put on a self within the reach of the poor and uneducated preaching of smooth things does not assail the wrong. Smooth things are in demand and he will never be taking to the brow of the precipice and cast down, he will never be commanded to "preach no more in his name." He will not be imprisoned for preaching Christ. That is not all bad; but the worst thing is this. He will not put one soul through heaven's gate and he himself will be cast down and not be privileged to stand in the congregation of the righteous. We must believe in what we say and do. Don't do eye service to please men. Have a sure message, void of social chatter. Know in whom you believe. If the truth is unpopular, preach it anyway, if it brings persecution and rejection count your blessings, you have joined forces with Peter, James and John.

They refuse to play it safe and speak a flowery message to appeal to the people and be free from the blood of all men. If they fail, let it not be; because they listened to a false message, however presumptuous this may sound; but let us not be put to shame by Peter, John, Paul, Stephen, Titus, and the others. In PROVERVS 3:5-12 "Trust in the Lord with all thine heart, and lean not unto thine own understanding. 6 in all thy ways acknowledge him, and he shall direct thy paths. 7 be not wise in thing own eyes, fear the Lord, and depart from evil. 8 it shall be health to the navel and marrow to thy bones. 9 honor the Lord with thy substance, and with the first fruits of all thy increase. 10 So shall thy barns be filled with plenty, and thy presses shall burst out with new wine. 11 my son, despise not the chastening of the Lord, neither be weary of his correction. 12 for whom the Lord loveth he correcteth, even as a father the son in whom he delighteth.

In the book of ROMANS 8:35-39 God is conqueror-that is what the resurrection declares. God is conqueror-that is what life confirms. The faith by which we live is faith in a conqueror God. He loses no battle in which he joins. He fears no enemy in which he is committed, and he finishes everything that he undertakes to do. If God has called you, don't spend time looking over your shoulders to see who is following; because it is God who leads and it is he who makes choice of those that are to follow.

THOUGHTS

Man is not always what he thinks he is but always what he thinks, he is. The comma makes the difference. This is the meaning of the biblical statements, for as he thinketh in his heart; so is he: PROVERBS 23:7. "Keep thy heart with all diligence, for out of it are the issues of life" PROVERBS 4:23. What is in view here is not thinking as a logic exercise. It is the whole of the innermost life. In the Bible, the heart alone is not the seed of the affections; it is the total thinking, feelings, and choices of the person–the focus of the mind and will and the fountain of life. There are some very practical conclusions that follow from those facts. What we think—in this broad sense of entertaining within our conscious attention—we are.

One of the most obvious consequences is the need to guard the gates of the soul against the poison of the evil imagination. The fact of evil is in this world, this we cannot avoid. What we need not do is to needlessly expose ourselves to it or entertain it within our minds. 1 THESSALONIANS 5:22 "Abstain from all appearance of evil. 23 And the very God of peace, sanctify you wholly, and I pray God, your whole spirit, soul, mind and body; be preserved blameless unto the coming of our Lord Jesus Christ. The obscene and the vile can be communicated through almost any media. It can come in the conversation by the printed page in photographs or pictures, via radio, motion pictures, and the television. Nobody regardless of age can afford to feed his mind and imagination or moral garbage. The Federal government lends a feeble effort to censor material by attempting to rate movies, magazines, and broadcast language.

The Federal communication commission (FCC) attempts to control radio and television, but the standards with which they judge are not the standards exemplified by the Holy Bible. You must be the censor department and suppress all repugnant material. This suppression exercise must be relinquished applied to the visual as well as the thought process. In MATTHEW 12:43 when the unclean spirit is gone out of a man, he walketh through dry places, seeking rest, and findeth none. 44 then he saith, I will return into my house from whence I came out. 45 then goeth him, and taketh with himself seven other spirits more wicked than himself, and they enter in and dwell there: and the last state of that man is worse than the first. Even so shall it be also unto this wicked generation. What Jesus was saying of a nation or a generation is equally true of an individual. We are most successful in excluding the evil by filling our minds and our lives with good thoughts. It is the idle mind "that is the devil workshop.

This same truth is put in these words by the Apostle Paul to the Philippians church: PHILIPPIANS 4:8 finally, brethren whatsoever things are true, whatsoever things are honest, whatsoever things are just, whatsoever things are pure, whatsoever things are lovely, whatsoever things are of good report; if there be any virtue, and if there be any praise, think on these things. 9 those things which you have both learned and received, and heard, and seen in me, do. And the God of peace shall be with you. The mind cannot act without something to act upon. One cannot think about something of which he is not aware of; for this reason the mind must feed with wholesome food. The wrong mental diet can cause serious problems. It is estimated three million in our world die each year of malnutrition. Many more millions are perishing because of malnutrition; in the mind and soul, that is fed nothing but husks; which cannot survive.

Fasting on husk may bring some sensation of fullness; but there is no nourishments for the whole man. In the book of JAMES 1:21-25 wherefore lay apart all filthiness and superfluity of naughtiness and received with meekness the engrafted word, which is able to save your soul. 22 but be ye doers of the word and not hearers only, deceiving your own selves. 23 for if any be a hearer of the word and not a doer, he is like unto a man beholding his natural face in a glass. 24 for he beholdeth himself, and goeth his way, and straightway forgetteth what manner of man he was. 25 but whosoever looketh into the perfect law of liberty, and continueth therein, he being not a forgetful hearer, but a doer of the word, this man shall be blessed in his deed.

That man shall not live by bread alone, but by every word of God which is affirmed in both the Old Testament and the New Testament. Man may exist as a physical sub-existence level until he is quite old. If he has made no provisions for his soul salvation and he dies and the memory of him is forgotten. We interpret that to mean that he has not merit a resurrection; he survived until old age on bread alone, but what do it profit a man if he should gain the whole world and lose his soul? The outer man is saved or sustained by bread but the hidden man of the heart is sustained and saved by the word of God. Jesus said, in JOHN 6:50-51 this is the bread which cometh down from heaven, that a man may eat thereof, and not die. 51 I am the living bread, which came down from heaven, if any man eat of this bread, he shall live forever, and the bread that I will give is my flesh, which I will give for the life of the world.

In view of this fact that which man thinketh in his heart, it is all important that one guard the gates of his soul, and that he supply his mind with the kind of mental diet needed to make one strong and able to endure hardness as a good soldier. I have been under this great teaching and have been instructed to write and record those truths and memorize them, and plant them into my mind as it said in St. Luke 9:44 let these sayings sink down deep into your ears; for the Son of man shall be delivered into the hands of men. Jesus knew he would soon be leaving them; so he was preparing them for his departure. I also knew when my pastor told us that if we had a church building then things would have to be set up like our other churches that have the people and facilities to conduct services like the other churches throughout our section of the 'Body of Christ' that this was prime time, that you can ask questions on the subject that he taught on Saturday night services, when we met in homes to be taught the word of God in its purest form with no contradictions.

Every six weeks they would have minister meetings where all our ministers and pastors would go to one of our main churches to discuss the scriptures in sincerity to make sure everybody come up with the same interpretation, understanding and explanation to the scriptures.

They work hard in seeking the truth to build a body of people in the true teachings of Jesus and the twelve Apostles, many times our pastor has come back with a scripture that has been upgraded or refine. And sometime a new revelation or a scripture or passage of a scriptures; we have been taught every aspect of the word of God, even commons, and periods sometimes can be placed in the wrong place and sometime the translator may place a period at the end of a chapter, when the thought has continued into the next chapter and that in itself can place a different meaning or explanation on the scripture. We are our best critic of anything; of anything not done correctly in the church or church grounds. Those issues are brought up and corrected. For a people to have such a love for the word of God and the truth entail the foundation that has been laid in our life; since 1913; when God called our leader to preach the pure and unadulterated word of God.

And God gave him the message of HAGGAI 2:9 the glory of this latter house shall be greater than of the former saith the Lord of hosts and in this place will I give peace, saith the Lord of hosts. The former was the New Testament church which lasted forty years, from Jesus ministry, which started at thirty years of age and the Apostles planted the churches and taught them the doctrines and teachings of the Holy Scriptures until they were martyrs for the gospel of Jesus; which ended 70 A.D. when Titus and his Roman army came into the city of Jerusalem and destroy it and even tore up the floor in the temple looking for gold and scatter the Nation of Israel to the four corners of the earth and they ceased to be a nation again until 1947. And the latter church will close the Gentiles supremacy in the first 7 ½ years prior to the battle or Armageddon in Revelation 16:16 and he gathered them together into a place called in the Hebrew tongue Armageddon. The latter church will be restore to finished its fulfillment in working in a perfect working order to finished the work the former church inaugurated before those God Anointed Apostles were martyr for the gospel dispensation.

And it is contained in the book of Revelations explains what God gave to our founder who had a divine calling by God to preach my gospel and this is the truth we have been working on in restoring the church exactly like the New Testament Church and we have not deviated from the faith; but we have continued to do so, with those truths that has been planted in our biblical heart which is our mind. The former church started in the upper room; with a hundred and twenty people preparing their lives and getting everything straighten out; before the Holy Spirit fell on them on the fiftieth day of wheat harvest of souls (people) speaking in a heavenly language as it said in ACTS 2: 1-4 and when the day of Pentecost was fully come, they were all with one accord in one place. 2 and suddenly there came a sound from heaven as of a rushing mighty wind; and it filled the entire house where they were sitting. 3 and there appeared unto them cloven tongues like as of fire, and it sat upon each of them. 4 and they were all filled with the Holy Spirit, and began to speak with other tongues as the Spirit gave them utterance.

This is when the church was inaugurated and brought forth; on the day of Pentecost. And the same Holy Spirit is prevalent in my life; and that is why God through his beloved son Jesus Christ and his righteousness has enabled me to go where nobody has achieved before; both Christians and non- Christians has witness the power of the Holy Spirit as it has manifested itself in me. I am Michigan Capital City (Lansing, Michigan) First 'BLACK' "Boxer of the Year" and New Al VanNess 'Appreciation Trophy' and made 'Sports Memories' By Jim Wallington 'Sports Writer' Lansing State Journal '1966.' from '1947' until '1966' I always mention Al VanNess who was a Professional Boxer, Trainer, Coach and Golden Gloves boxing Promoter; since he told me they did not want to give you 'Boxer of the Year' since I was 'BLACK' he said he told them I should have won it every year that I had boxed and that was from 1964, 1965, and 1966.

I became a Born again Christian in the Non-Denominational Pentecostal Church on September 5, 1972. I believe I have a calling on my life through Jesus Christ, God's only begotten son; to witness in giving the Testimony I have been blessed with to give to the world of man-kind, or sinners; for the hope of abiding with him throughout the seedless and endless ages of eternity.

ALZHEIMER'S BEDRIDDEN - HEALINGS AND MIRACLES

In 2 KINGS 5:1 NOW Naaman, captain of the host of the king of the host of the king of Syria, was a great man with his master and honorable, because by him the Lord had given deliverance unto Syria, he was also a mighty man in valor, but he was a leper. 2 and the Syrians had gone out by companies, and had brought away captives out of the land of Israel a little maid, and she waited on Naaman's wife. 3 and she said unto her mistress, would God my Lord were with the prophet that is in Samaria; for he would recover him from his leprosy. 4 and one went in, and told his Lord, saying, thus said the maid that is of the land of Israel. 5 and the king of Syria said, go to and I will send a letter unto the king of Israel, and he departed, and took with him ten talents of silver, and six thousand pieces of gold, and ten changes of raiment. 6 and he brought the letter to the king of Israel, saying now when this letter is come unto thee, behold I have therewith sent Naaman my servant to thee, that thou mayest recover him of his leprosy.

7 and it came to pass, when the king of Israel had read the letter, that he rent his clothes, and said, am I God, to kill and to make alive, that this man doth send unto me to recover a man of his leprosy? Wherefore consider, I pray for you, and see how he seeketh a quarrel against me. 8 and it was so; when Elisha the man of God had heard that the king of Israel had rent his clothes; that he sent to the king, saying wherefore hast thou rent thy clothes, that he sent to the king, saying, wherefore hast thou rent thy clothes: let him, come now to me, and he shall know that there is a prophet in Israel.

9 so Naaman came with his horses and with his chariot, and stood at the door of the house of Elisha. 10 and Elisha sent a messenger

unto him; saying; go and wash in Jordan seven times, and thy flesh shall come again to thee, and thou shalt be clean. 11 but Naaman was wroth and went away, and said, behold I thought he would surely come out to me, and stand, and call on the name of the Lord his God, and strike his hand over the place, and recover the leper. 12 are not Abana and Pharpar, rivers of Damascus, better than all the waters of Israel? May I not wash in them, and be clean? So he turned and went away in a rage. 13 and his servants came near, and spoke unto him, and said, my father, if the prophet had bid thee to do some great thing, wouldest thou not have done it? How much rather then, when he saith to thee, wash and be clean?

14 then went him down, and dipped himself seven times in the river Jordan, according to the saying of the man of God and his flesh came again like unto the flesh of a little child, and he was clean. 15 and he returned to the man of God, he and all his company, and came, and stood before him, and he said, behold, now I know that there is no God in all the earth, but in Israel. Now therefore, I pray thee, take a blessing of thy servant.

16. But he said, as the Lord liveth, before whom I stand, I will receive none. And he urged him to take it; but he refused. 17 and Naaman said; shall there not then, I pray thee, be given to thy servant two mules, burden of the earth: For thy servant will henceforth do not offer nor sacrifice unto other gods, but unto the Lord. 18 in this thing the Lord pardon thy servant, that when my master goeth into the house of Rimmon to worship there, and he leaneth on my hand, and I bow down myself in the house of Rimmon, the Lord pardon thy servant in this thing. 19 and he said unto him, go in peace. So he departed from him a little way. 20 but Gehazi, the servant of Elisha the man of God, said, behold my master hath spared Naaman this Syrian, in not receiving at his hand, that which he brought, but as the Lord liveth, I will run after him, and take some what of him. 21 so Gehazi followed after Naaman, and when Naaman saw him running, after him, he lighted down from the chariot to meet him, and said, is all well?

22 and he said, all is well. My master hath sent me, saying, behold, even now there become to me from mount Ephraim two young men

of the sons of the prophets, give them I pray thee, a talent of silver and two changes of garments. 23 and Naaman said, be content, take two talents, and he urged him, and bound two talents of silver in two bags, with two change of garments, and laid them upon two of his servants, and they bare them before him. 24 and when he came to the tower, he took them from their hand, and bestowed them in the house; and he let the men go, and they departed. 25 but he went in, and stood before his master; and Elisha said unto him, whence comest thou, Gehazi? And he said, thy servant went no whither. 26 and he said unto him, went not mine heart with thee, when the man turned again from his chariot to meet thee? Is it a time to receive garments and olive yards, and vineyards, and sheep, and oxen, and men servants, and maid servants.

27 the leprosy therefore of Naaman shalt cleave unto thee and unto thy seed forever. And he went out from his presence, a leper as white as snow. I also believe there can be generation blessings, as a result of the favor my Mother found in the eyes of the Lord through her faithfulness to God and his beloved son Jesus Christ. And I believe that is the main reason my Mother knew I was going to be baptize in the Holy Spirit with the evidence of speaking in a heavenly language as it is stated in the book of ACTS 2:4 and they were all filled with the Holy Spirit, and began to speak with other tongues, as the Spirit gave them utterance. And my oldest sister had a dream that I was being filled with the precious Holy Spirit. The Holy Scriptures said in MATTHEW 18:16 but if he will not hear thee, then take with thee one or two more, that in the mouth of two or three witnesses every word may be established.

And the Holy Spirit was confirmed in my life on September 5, 1972, when I was baptize in the Holy Spirit; and began to speak in a heavenly language, as the Spirit gave me utterance with the evidence of speaking in a heavenly language. The Spirit is life is what God is because he is life. It's just like the sun, there is only one sun in this universe; but the rays of the sun can be felt all over the universe. The same way God's Holy Spirit works; it dwells in our mind, in the secret recesses of the mind or heart and it goes throughout our nervous systems that is why I can fill it throughout my body.

The second example in 1KINGS 17:1-24 and Elijah the Tishbite, who was of the inhabitants of Gilead, said unto Ahab, as the Lord God of Israel liveth, before whom I stand, there shall not be dew or rain these years; but according to my word. 2 and the word of the Lord came unto him, saying. 13 get thee hence, and turn thee eastward, and hide thyself by the brook Cherith; that is before Jordan. 4 and it shall be; that thou shalt drink of the brook; and I have commanded the ravens to feed thee there. 5 so he went and did according to the word of the Lord; for he went and dwell by the brook Cherith; that is before Jordan. 6 and the ravens brought him bread and flesh in the morning, and bread and flesh in the evening; and he drank of the brook. 7 and it came to pass after a while, that the brook dried up, because there had been no rain in the land. 8 and the word of the Lord came unto him, saying. 9 arise, get thee to Zarephath, which belongeth to Zidon, and dwell there, behold, I have commanded a widow woman there to sustain thee. 10 so he arose and went to Zarephath. And when he came to the gate of the city behold, the widow woman was there gathering of sticks, and he called to her, and said fetch me, I pray thee, a little water in a vessel, that I may drink.

11 and as she was going to fetch it, he called to her, and said, bring me I pray the, a morsel of bread in thine hand. 12 and she said, as the Lord liveth, I have not a cake, but an handful of meal in a barrel, and a little oil in a cruse; and behold, I am gathering two sticks, that I may go in and dress it for me and my son, that we may eat it, and die. 13 and Elijah said unto her; fear not, go and do as thou hast said, but make me thereof a little cake first, and bring it unto me, and after make for thee and for thy son. 14 for thus saith the Lord God of Israel. The barrel of meal shall not waste; neither shall the cruse of oil fail, until the day that the Lord sendeth upon the earth. 15 and she went and did according to the saying of Elijah, and she, and he, and her house, did eat many days. 16 and the barrel of meal wasted not, neither did the cruse of oil fail, according to the word of the LORD, which he spoke by Elijah. 17 And it came to pass after these things; that the son of the woman, the mistress of the house, fell sick; and his sickness was so sore; that there was no breath left in him.

18 And she said unto Elijah; what have I to do with thee, O thou man of God: art thou come unto me to call my son to remembrance, and to slay my son? 19 And he said unto her, give me thy son. And he took him out of her bosom, and carried him up into a loft, where he abode, and laid him upon his own bed. 20 And he cried unto the LORD, and said, O LORD my God, hast thou also brought evil upon the window with whom I sojourn, by slaying her son? And he stretched himself upon the child, three times, and cried unto the LORD, and said, O LORD my God, I pray thee, let this child's soul come into him again. 22 And the Lord heard the voice of Elijah; and the soul of the child came into him again, and he revived. 23 And Elijah took the child, and brought him down out of the chamber into the house, and delivered him unto his Mother; And Elijah said, see, thy son liveth. 24 And the woman said to Elijah now by this" I know that thou art a man of God, and that the word of the LORD in thy mouth is truth. Then in ST. LUKE 4:27 and many lepers were in Israel in the time of Eliseus the Prophet; and none of them was cleanse, saving Naaman the Syrian.

I am very grateful and appreciative in what The Lord is doing in my life. And what He has continued to manifest Himself in signs and wonders following His Holy word. Though a chosen vessel that hast been sanctified or set apart for His Holy use. And God has blessed me exceedingly above many my own equal that have been taught by our Ministry who have study and research the bible in truth and righteousness. And have planted those truths into our minds. And it was as a result of those truths being imparted into my life, through the experiences through sharing in Jesus Christ suffering; as Apostle Paul said in PHILIPPIANS 3:10 -15 that I may know him, and the power of His resurrection, and the fellowship of his sufferings, being made conformable unto his death. 11. If by any means I might attain unto the resurrection of the dead. 12 Not as though I had already attained, either were already perfect; but I follow after; if that I may apprehend that for which also I am apprehended of Christ Jesus.

13 Brethren, I count not myself to have apprehended; but this one thing I do; forgetting those things which are behind, and reaching forth unto those things which are before. 14 I press toward the mark

for the prize of the high calling of God in Christ Jesus. 15 Let us therefore; as many as be perfect; be thus minded; and if in anything ye be thus otherwise minded, God shall reveal even this unto you. I have truly proven myself to God; and His beloved son Jesus Christ. And that is why this second book that is a continuation from the first book (Boxer of the Year Hudson VGM).

ALZHEMER'S APPOINTMENT

The first appointment I had to see Dennis M. Pelon PhD P.C. Neuropsychology and Rehabilitation Services 1640 Haslett, Road Suite 110, Haslett, Michigan 48840; was on Monday, June 23, 2008 at 8:30 A.M. I was in his office approximately four hours; after the testing or diagnosis, he told me that I had Alzheimer's and in seven years I would be bedridden; but my taking the medication it would slow it down a couple of years. And he wanted to see me again in one to two years. I was to continue to see Doctor Hilton Thomas my Psychologist, and Doctor William T. BeeCroft, M.D. BOARD CERTIFIED PSYCHIATRY.

HISTORY: He has a long standing history of depression, suicidal, ideation, and preoccupation with past life events. He also has been experiencing changes in memory and cognition and there are concerns regarding development of a dementia process. He has also been experiencing changes in memory and cognition and there are concerns regarding development of a dementia process. He has since 1983 experience suicidal ideation, and this begun occurring sometime after he filed a Civil Rights lawsuit against General Motors, where he was employed for nearly thirty years until 1994. He did not prevail in his first lawsuit, and the expense of this undertaking resulted in significant financial stress. He has recently obtained an MRI scan of the brain; showing apparent small vessel white matter ischemic changes in per ventricular region as well as some mild atrophy. He has a medical history significant concussion, the first experience as the result of a bicycle accident around the age of ten; which resulted in loss of consciousness with post- traumatic amnesia of approximately half hour, and between 1964 and 1969 he was a Golden Gloves boxer and experience one clean episode of loss of consciousness and the result of head trauma and was dazed multiple times. He also was drafted into the U.S. ARMY in the Special Services on the Third U.S. Army Boxing Team, at Fort McClellan in Anniston, Alabama where he was a 125 pound Featherweight Boxing Champion that qualified him to go to the Third U.S. ARMY Boxing Tournament at Fort Campbell, Kentucky where he was nominated for the All Army Boxing Team.

Then he was shipped to Cam Ranh Bay, Viet Nam. He has been diagnosed with sleep Apnea and utilizes a CPAP. He otherwise is without CNS impacting disease or conditions including major vessel CVA'S alcohol or substance abuse, neurotoxin exposure, seizures, high fevers, tumors, or family history of Neurological conditions. He was educated to the Associate Degree level in Philosophy; he has been married for thirty years with three children, ages twenty-eight, twenty-six, and twenty, who are doing fine. Current concerns and reason for Neuropsychological evaluation are to rule out an early dementia process vs. Pseudo dementia associated with depression and to assist with treatment planning process. The above medical information and history are considered essential for purposes of test interpretation, diagnostic, and report formulation.

TEST RESULTS: Attention and information processing capabilities showed signs of substantial impairment. His simple attention and mental tracking tested intact on the mental control subtest where he was able to perform reversed digit counting, alphabet recitation, and serial three's with only two errors (twenty-fifth Percentile). Nonetheless, Tests requiring more complex attention, mental set shifting, and information processing speed revealed prominent deficits. When performing simple visual scanning and tracking of a single sequence of numbers, he demonstrated loss of mental set and began connecting the numbers at random, and needed prompting and cueing to resume the sequential scanning and tracking with the trial making Test-Part A completed in one, one nine with performance below the one percentile.

His ability to alternate or shift attention between ongoing sequences of events and maintain place in the previous sequence also tested as profoundly impaired with The Trial Making Test-Part B completed in three thirty nine (below one percentile). During the later task; he required prompting and cueing to continue connecting the number and letters with a continuous line, and again self-direction of attention focus was found to be quite limited. He requires external prompting and cueing. His information processing speed with a psychomotor component also tested below normal on the Symbol Digit Mutability Test, Written Form, with only twenty number letter pairings accomplished in the ninety trial with performance below the one percentile for age and education His visual information processing speeds not requiring a motor response were at the ninth percentile for word recognition, color recognition was at the second percentile on the Strop Test relative to age and education-appropriate norms. In short this patient demonstrates profound limitations in cognition efficiency alternation of attention, and complex attention abilities, while simple attention and mental tracking remain intact.

Memory and New learning capabilities tested with evidence of substantiate impairment. He demonstrated difficulty with encoding, retention, and retrieval processed identified. His ability to recall conversational details was at the one percentile during immediate recall seventeen fifty and at thirty minutes delay, recall was at the ninth Percentile ten\ fifty on the Wechsler Memory   Scale-Revised Logical Memory   subtest. There were   or embellishment of the material presented his association without realizing it. Accuracy of recall can be an issue. His verbal learning process was found to be below normal with acquisition across three learning trails at the fifth Percentile nineteen/ thirty six recall at twenty five minutes delay was at the one percentile five/twelve and recognition recall was at the one percentile utilizing a multitude-choice format seven twelve relative to age appropriate norms on the Hopkins Verbal Learning Test. His retention rate for newly acquired information was at forty-four percent, which is below the one percentile for his age on the latest test. Visual spatial memory was similarly found to be below normal range expectations with only seven/thirty-six units of visual detail and spatial location information adequately encoded into immediate memory below one percentile on the Brief Visual-Spatial Memory Test, while recall at twenty-five minutes also was below the one percentile 11/12 and recognition recall utilizing a multiple-choice format was at the four percentile three/six. The retention rate of thirty percentile was below the first percentile for the initially encoded visual-spatial information.

Visual-Spatial Memory was more thoroughly evaluated with thirty-minute delay recall on the Regulated Complex Figure Test at 2/36 seventh Percentile with visual memory span testing revealed low normal level performances with five digits forward and four in reverse, sixteen percentile; with visual span at a sequence of five forward and three in reverse, sixteen percentile. In short, this patient demonstrates substantial impairment in the ability to form new memories and retain new information after a delay with both auditory- verbal and visual Non Verbal Memory Functions Significantly Affected. Higher Cognitive Functions including Conceptual Reasoning, Problem Solving, cognitive Flexibility, initiation, planning, and self-monitoring capabilities showed signs of selective impairment. Conceptual reasoning when language medication was involved tested intact on the Wisconsin Card Sorting.

Test-64 with performance revealing three categories obtained. There were only twenty three preservative responses, placing performance at the ninth percentile for cognitive rigidity. His ability to generate ideas, plan, and initiate also tested intact on language-based measures including verbal fluency or word generation capacity on the Controlled Oral Word Association test with performance obtaining the twenty percentile, while category Fluency Test results were at the sixty percentile. None-the-less, there was deficiency identified in his ability to generate ideas, plan, and initiate on The Ruff Figural Fluency Test with performance at the fifth percentile for initiation and productive thinking capabilities, while cognitive Flexibility was clearly impaired with the Perseveration Index exceedingly the ninety nine percentile. His number of perseverations outnumbered the unique designs he generated such that he readily became entrenched in his own ideas and was unable to self-identify when he was perseverating or reiterating the same spatial configurations and designs on this test of non-verbal planning and initiation.

His planning and sequential reasoning capabilities tested at the eight percentile on the tower of London Test, where speed of problem solving was normal range at the eighteen percentile and self, monitoring capabilities were also well preserved at the twenty fourth percentile. Speech and language functions tested with evidence of dysphasia. He demonstrated some mild dysarthria and difficulty articulating two third screening words, and there was some mild difficulty; with auditory-verbal comprehension and mental calculation observed as well. Boston naming Test results, in fact, revealed evidence of dysphasia or difficulty naming common objects from memory with a score of forty-one sixty obtaining the one "percentile relative to age appropriate norms. His verbal comprehension did test below normal with regards to the ability to decipher meaning from sentence structure and comprehend propositional speech when token test results at the first percentile thirty-four/ forty four.

Sensory perceptual examination revealed significant suppression in tactile perceptual function, more on the left than right. In fact, graph aesthesia testing revealed four errors in the finger tip number writing procedure on the right and eight on the left reflecting marked difficulty revisualizing numbers traced on the skin. His mental imagery for numbers appears to be significantly affected. His tactile perfection during double simultaneous stimulation of hand and face also revealed bilateral suppression with four errors on the right and four on the left. Visual fields were full to confrontation testing. There was no dystercognosis or difficulty identifying shape by sense of touch. Higher level measure of visual spatial perception tested as clearly impaired. He had marked difficulty judging direction and distance with judgment of line Orientation Test results at the first percentile fifteen thirty. Object perception and pattern recognition were at the third percentile on the Silhouettes subtest thirteen thirty.

Motor function assement revealed normal range simple motor speed and dexterity but below-normal level constructional praxis. He demonstrated normal range simple motor speed on the finger Oscillation Test with forty-six four taps/ten on the right (seventy percentile and forty four and four taps/ ten: on the left seventy fifth percentile. Dominant hand superiority was demonstrated on the

Purdue Pegboard Teat with thirteen pegs correctly placed, eleven by the non-dominant left hand, and ten during bimanual performance, all exceeding the cutoff scores such that normal range performance was observed. He demonstrated substantial construction dyspraxia with marked difficulty spatially organizing and assembling objects with Block Design subtest results at the second percentile and Regular Complex Figure Test Copy Phase results at the fifth percentile (twenty- four/thirty-six).

The Personality Assessment Inventory was completed by the patient, but an invalid profile was obtained. The patient presented himself in a bad light, endorsing an abnormally high level of negative attributes symptoms, and traits, exceeding the ninety-ninth percentile, and in fact exceeding the patient sample norms. His responses to the test were characterized by an inconsistent pattern of responding, which also exceeded the ninety-ninth percentile. Clearly this patient has difficulty understanding and characterizing his clinical symptomatology at present, or has some motivational to distort self- presentation.

SUMMARY: This male with average range of intellectual development and remote history of concussion, sleep apnea, and approximately twenty year treatment for depression and an obsession preoccupation with past life events demonstrates evidence of significant generalized cognitive decline; not fully explained by normal aging or depression. Current test results points to substantial deterioration in the ability to form new memories and retain new information after a delay accompanied by low normal performances on measures of complex attention, mental set shifting, and self-direction of attention, mental set shifting, and self-direction of attention process. His ability to initiate, plan, name common objects from memory, verbal comprehension of propositional speech, object perfection, spatial perception of direction, graphesthesia or ability to revisualize symbols traced on the skin and constructional praxis tested below normal consistent with a fluency, conceptual reason such as language-based or mediated remain well preserved and retained.

The patient has normal range immediate for auditory and visual sequence as well. Personality assessment revealed a tendency to present himself in a "bad light" and an invalid profile was obtained with the self-report inventory utilized. Clearly, this patient has a long standing history of depression and obsession thought process. Diagnostically, current test results and history are consistent with a Dementia NOS (three thirty one and nine) which likely has an Alzheimer's component. A Global Deterioration Rating Scale Score of five/seven is suggested.

RECOMMENDATIONS: 1. this patient, is in likely hood, would benefit from a cholinesterase inhibitor and antiglutamatergic medication aimed at slowing the functional decline and deterioration associated with what appears to be an Alzheimer's dwoisease process. 2. This patient is in need of assistance with decision making, and in fact his ability to comprehend new and unfamiliar information, plan, initiate, shift mental set, and retain new and unfamiliar information accurately for purposes of providing informed consent is severely limited by the dementia process. A Durable Power of Attorney arrangement at minimum is needed, and in fact a guardianship conservatorship would also be appropriate if a suitable Durable Power Of Attorney arrangement cannot be accomplished. The patient would do best, however, to maintain input into decision making so as to maintain some sense of control providing him with a menu of options but with the final decision made by the Durable Power Of Attorney.

3. Regularly schedule social and recreational activities are needed. This patient is unable to sufficiently plan, self structure, and follow through with a sufficient range of activities to maintain an ethylic mood. 4. This patient likely would benefit from engaging in activities aimed at increasing cortical reserve and stimulating metabolic activity in temporal and partial lobe regions. A brief handout will be provided to the patient for this purpose. 5. Owing to marked limitations in memory and mental act shifting capabilities, supervision and monitoring of his medications, nutritional intake, and safety needs is needed. 6. Owing to substantial limitations in information processing speed, mental set shifting spatial perception of direction increased susceptibility to distraction and visual scanning

speed and on the road driving evaluation is recommended to issue driving safety.

7. A repeat Neuropsychological evaluation is recommended in one year to monitor for stabilization of his condition and/or further neurocognitive decline and to update the current recommendations. On my second evaluation on January 20, 2011 after the testing, he had me to go into the waiting area and he would come and get me when he had the results. About thirty minutes later he came back in to get me for the results. He said your condition is steadily deteriorating and he did not want me driving without a professional driver, riding with me to see if I was capable of driving alone and he wanted to see me again in one to two years to see if I needed Supervision.

I went to our Church Convention over the Labor Day weekend in Louisville, Kentucky. I said prior to going to the meeting I was going to do more in that meeting in testifying and worshiping and praising the Lord, than I have ever done since my inception of receiving the Holy Spirit into the deepest recesses of the heart (mind) which is where it dwells; which is your bible mind and you can feel it throughout your body; because it works through our nervous systems and that's why our body was made for the purpose of the indwelling of the Holy Spirit and God design it that way when He created Adam and saw it was not good for man to be alone so he created him a help mate (EVE) and not a headache by causing a deep sleep to come over Adam and took a rib out of Adam and made him a woman; because she was taking out of man to help him and not to rule over him, but for him to be the head of his household.

I had just recently been connected to face book in promoting my first book 'Boxer of the Year' Hudson VGM; where I went through a campaign promotion where one of the features was having an interview from a radio station from North East Texas where I gave several testimonies which led me to write another book to culminate with the first book. I explained the results of my Healings, Miracles, and the seventeen year's Civil Rights Lawsuit against the number one Automaker in the world General Motors in Lansing, Michigan at Plant 1, where I worked in the Inspection Audit Department. It all started on August 19, 1983 and I am still writing about it; because of the many blessings that has been bestowed upon my life through the Holy Spirit which is the life of God. In the book of Saint John 4:24 God is a Spirit, and they that worship him must worship him in spirit and in truth.

There are two Spirits there's one with a upper case 'S' and the other with a lower case's'. Here's how we interpret that scripture: God is a Spirit; eternal being and He seek other beings to worship him in spirit and that is with their life and it must be done with truth. He does not seek ghosts to worship him; but spirit beings with form and flesh and blood). There was a certain young girl named Ravon, who looked like she was about sixteen or eighteen years old; and had cancer and had several relapses and was hospitalized several times and she was so sick from taking Chemotherapy. I was so touched by her condition.

I told this woman who had her on face book, and asked the Christians on face book to pray for her. I sent her an e-mail and told her I would be praying for Ravon at our Church Convention in Louisville Kentucky, over the Labor Day weekend. I drove their myself and after arriving there Thursday; before the first Friday morning service I checked in at the Church and was assigned a room at the Church Convention Center with about ten beds in each room and the rooms are free and also the dining room staff prepares the meals which are very nutritional and everything is free before the morning services and after the afternoon services and after the evening services we go out to one of the restaurants in the city; for a night time snack before returning to our rooms or motels for the night.

I went to McDonald to use their WIFI for my laptop computer and when I turned to my e-mails and I went to my face book page on my timeline. There was a picture of the young cancer patient, and Kanika Starr Reynolds said she was in so much pain and there was nothing that she could do. I sent her a message to let her know that I would be praying for her, that I was dedicating the whole three days of service to Ravon. I pray to the Lord Jesus to let him know I was going to do more than I have in these three days of our Church Convention than I have ever done since I have been filled with The Holy Spirit; with the evidence of speaking in a heavenly language.

The way they received it on the day of Pentecost in the book of ACTS 2:4 which is the church in action; when the New Testament Church was launched or came into existence.

During the night service which started at 7: P.M. in the evening. I testify, worship and praised the Lord with dance and song to the glory of God. There was an atmosphere there for some great Spiritual blessing from the Lord. And the showers of blessings were there. The Bishop and the pastors and ministers were singing and praising the Lord. Then the men started coming up to the altar on the right side and the women moved out to the left side of the altar, the men and women are separated when coming up to the front of the altar to be prayed for by the ministry. The ministry was laying hands on the saints, and some was crying with tears of joy; as it said in the book of PSALMS 126: 5 they that sow in tears shall reap with joy. They were reaping the benefits of heaven and you could feel the present of the Holy Spirit in our midst and the saints were responding in dancing, shouting, worshiping and praising the Lord. I was speaking in a heavenly language both with my understanding and in the Holy Spirit making intercession for me to the Father and the Holy Spirit moving over me like the Apostle and Prophets and the saints in the New Testament Church.

When we were singing while sitting on the pews or benches the Holy Spirit began to move. And the leader or the pastor of the Convention Center stood up then all the ministers, then their wives and the congregation. And every time I would look up at the screen; for the words of the song, the tears began to roll down my face and I had to turn my head away for the beautiful Spiritual words; which were so heavenly; to keep from crying out loud. Then I would look at the screen again and start back singing and those heavenly words would bring tears to my eyes again and I would have to stop singing and turn my face away from the screen. And it went on like this through the duration of the song. After the service before I went out to a restaurant or fast food business I had to take a shower and change clothes for my suit and dress shirt was soak and wet. I think we were on the floor for about two hours rejoicing in the Lord. I danced for about forty-five minutes to an hour and when I stopped dancing and raised my arm to praise the Lord, the Holy Spirit took over and began to move my hands and body it was that strong and powerful, that's when I know I have touched the throne of God and Jesus lets me feel his love by the Holy Spirit manifesting itself through me.

At McDonald with my new laptop; that I purchase from my Mothers Trust and having connected it to their WIFI and checking my e-mail and going to my timeline on face book and Ravon the girl I had dedicated the whole service to because of her cancer; and Kanika said they were going somewhere for recreation since the young girl felt better. And I have seen her on my timeline recently and she looks good. This is what my life for Christ is all about is living a life which is pleasing in his sight. When I have great prayers answered it do not surprise me because I have been taught and instructed how to live a Christ like life and how important it is to study the bible and all the books of history that supports the bible, for instance, a good Bible Concordance, Handbook, Dictionary and Vine Expository Dictionary of New Testament words of English and the Greek definition of words.

Then some great history books such as Foxe's Book of Martyrs, ROMAN CATHOLICISM, which is the oldest religion in the world after which the oldest religion in the world after the Christian era which started in the book of Acts; which is the true church in action which started out as a Jewish church, and then in ACTS 10:1-48 Through Cornelius a gentile became the first gentile God start dealing with; from then on the door was open to all people. The last day of the Church Convention which started at 10: A.M. in the morning, till about 2: P.M in the afternoon. A white brother was testifying to the glory of God in edifying the congregation; he was talking about an old car and a new car and compare it with our old body and our new body in Christ and how both contrast each other; but yet the same principle applies. After he finished the first thought that came to my mind was my 1972 Cutlass Convertible Oldsmobile; that I purchase brand new and I still have it and it still runs just like new.

I would like to see it fixed up just like I bought it brand new with Michigan State University colors of green and white convertible top and white pinstripes. The organist started a perfect song to end the

Convention with. "I see the cloud arising for the latter rain through God Ministry in Jesus name. It was about the Bride of Christ being taking up into third heaven; which the Tabernacle was a type of God dwelling in the third compartment; which was the Holies of Holies. In the book of PSALMS 75:6 for promotion cometh neither from the East, nor from the West, nor from the South, therefore the only direction left is North where God dwells and when the scriptures referring to Jerusalem; it refers to it as the North Country. And the Jewish people are God's chosen people and are located in a geographical location in that part of the country and right in the middle of Jerusalem is the abbreviation of the United States of America (USA). And we are the country God has chosen to protect his chosen people the Jewish nation.

In the book of Saint JOHN 4:22-26 ye worship ye know not what, we know what we worship; for salvation is of the Jews. 23 but the hour cometh and now is, when the true worshippers shall worship the Father in spirit and in truth: for the Father seeketh such to worship him. 24 God is a Spirit, and they that worship him must worship him in spirit and in truth. 25 the woman saith unto him, I know that Messiah; which is called Christ, when he is come he will tell us all things. (Jesus saith unto her, I that speak unto thee am he)." When the organist and choir director with the chorus, that brought the service to a high Spiritual plateau I was so touched I did a little dance about six yards up and about six yards back to my seat, which was the front row and I raised both of my hands and looked up toward heaven.

The Holy Spirit started moving my arms and hands just like when the wind is blowing the branches and the leaves on a tree. The Holy Spirit does the same thing. Just like in JOHN 3:1 THERE was a man of the Pharisees, named Nicodemus, a ruler of the Jews. 2 The same came to Jesus by night, and said unto him, Rabbi, we know that thou came to Jesus by night, and said unto him, Rabbi, we know that thou art a teacher come from God; for no man can do these miracles that thou doest except God be with him. 3. Jesus answered and said unto him verily, verily, I say unto thee, except a man be born again, he cannot see the kingdom of God. 4 Nicodemus saith unto him, how can a man be born when he is old? Can he enter the second time into his mother's womb and be born? 5 Jesus answered: Verily, verily, I say unto thee, except a man is born of water and of the Spirit, he cannot enter into the kingdom of God.

6. That which is born of the flesh is flesh; and that which is born of the Spirit is Spirit. 7 Marvel not that I said unto thee, ye must be born again. 8 The wind bloweth where it listeth, and thou hearest the sound, but cannot tell whence it cometh, and whiter it goeth, so is everyone that is born of the Spirit. 9 Nicodemus answered and said unto him, how can these things be? 10 Jesus answered and said unto him art thou a master in Israel, and knowest not these things. 11 Verily, verily, I say unto thee, we speak that we do know, and testify that we have seen; and ye receive not our witness. 12 If I have told you earthly things, and ye believe not, how shall ye believe, if I tell you of heavenly things? "Therefore when a person is born again they will know it for themselves and nobody has to tell them they have it; for they will know for themselves.

The pastor of the Convention Center said this is a good note to close out the services on a high note. And from now own it is going to get greater. I went to my room at the convention center and change into my traveling clothes to head back to Lansing, Michigan; after the usher that was in charge of praying and blessing the meal, and then dismiss the Saints by rows after the line has diminished then the next row etc. I am usually about the last person to eat since I go directly to my room in the Convention Center and pack all by belongings and get the bedding ready for those that are in charge of that department. Then I would take the luggage and briefcase to my car and then head to the dining room for a nice nutrition dinner. After finishing my dinner I walk to my car and set my GPS and attach it to the window shield.

After leaving the Church parking lot and driving down the street toward the exit to the expressway, with my tape on with a nice song which was one of my wife tapes she left in my car and I was just feeling so uplifted, encouraged, and inspired, with such a zeal and enthusiasm; for the things of God; and as soon as I drove on the exit on to the expressway. The Holy Spirit came upon me and the tears began to fall down my face and it started me to crying with so much joy and it began to move my upper body and I had complete control of my faculty's and this went on for about two to three minutes; then it would leave for about two to three minutes; then everything would be normal again. Then it would come on me again automatically; and it would cause me to cry and I did not stop it or quench the Holy Spirit; with all the love and heavenly joy for two or three minutes, then it would leave and everything would be back to normal with no tears or movement for two to three minutes.

This continued for about three hours from the time I looked at the time; and I also felt like speaking to the lord in a heavenly language with more tears of joy. I arrived home in about five hours; instead of the six to seven hours; then it dawn on me, this time I did not stop at the rest area or stop at McDonalds for a meal. I have made it to Louisville, Kentucky several times with a tank of gas; before leaving for Lansing, Michigan after the Church Convention. I knew that I was completely healed from the incurable disease of Alzheimer's that I was diagnosed with on 6/23/2008, and twenty-six years with High Blood Pressure. And twenty-six years under a Psychologist, and twenty-one years under a Psychiatrist, and at least seven Hospitalization's in mental Hospitals. The way the Holy Spirit came among me with a great love; on my way home from our annual Church Convention in Louisville, Kentucky; reminded me of when God chose Moses the great Prophet of God to lead his people out of Egypt to the promise land.

In the book of EXODUS 13: 20-21 and they took their journey from Succoth, and encamped in Etham; in the edge of the wilderness. 21 and the Lord went before them by day in a pillar of a cloud, to lead them the way; and by night in a pillar of fire, to give them light, to go by day and night. 2 He did not take away the pillar of cloud by day nor the pillar of fire by night, from before the people; therefore when the cloud moved the Israelites moved, when the cloud stopped, the people would stop. And this was similar to how the Holy Spirit came upon me, and it would move me and cause me to cry with tears of joy. And then the Holy Spirit would leave for two to three minutes; then everything was normal with no tears of joy for two to three minutes and it was so heavenly to have the Spirit of God to take complete control of my life.

And I knew through the Holy Spirit and how the Holy Spirit have worked in my life for forty years at that time since September 5, 1972, when I received the Baptism of the Holy Spirit; as it took place in the book of ACTS 10: 44 - 48 while Peter yet spoke these words, the Holy Spirit fell on all of them which heard the word. 45 And they of the circumcision which believed were astonished; as many as came with Peter, because that on the Gentiles also was poured out the gift of the Holy Spirit. 46 For they heard them speak with tongues, and magnify God. Then answer Peter. 47 Can any man forbid water; that these should not be baptized which have received the Holy Spirit as well as we? 48 And he commanded them to be baptized in the name of the Lord; then prayed they him to tarry certain days.

The events that happened and transpired that led to me being diagnosed with the incurable disease of Alzheimer's are in my first book "Boxer of the Year" Hudson VGM. I would like to talk about my New Book in detail, concerning the healings and miracles that I received after the Lord blessed me with the Civil Rights lawsuits, that the Department of Civil Rights in Lansing, Michigan, rejected it and I appealed it to the State appeal board in Detroit, Michigan and they rejected it; but they gave me the right to pursuit it in Circuit Court if I chose to do so within thirty days.

My first two attorneys was a husband and wife team asked me to fire them? I would not do it; so they asked Judge Thomas Brown to withdraw them from the case about two weeks before the case was set for trial. And he granted it. Therefore I had to find an attorney to represent me; so I had to hire another attorney for five thousand dollars. He asked the judge to postpone the lawsuit to give him enough time to go over the materials so he could be prepare to represent me. The judge refused and said it would take place on the date that had already been set for the case.

Therefore I had to represent myself. The Judge told me after the kangaroo court; that I did not have a Civil Rights case, and that General Motors had incurred some attorney fees and he asked Mr. William Schultz the attorney representing General Motors. How much have you incurred in attorney fees? He said about ten grand. He said Mr. Hudson you owe General Motors Ten thousand dollars and pointed his family at me in front of my wife and said, this will teach you to go against General Motors. The General Foreman that started the ordeal that the Holy Spirit led me to pursuit against General Motors, because of discrimination and because I was a Born Again Christian that believed in perfection like Jesus Christ came from outside into the Circuit Court room and shook their attorney hand and embrace him.

I went home with my wife and I got on my knees and prayed the prayer of faith to God through His beloved son Jesus Christ. And I prayed that God would bless me with the material that I needed to get me back in court. I was blessed with another lawsuit by the Holy Spirit, which also acts as an intercessor allowed me to find what I needed to get me back into court after filing another Civil Rights complaint, so I could at least recover my financial losses. I also prayed the Lord Jesus would make a way for me to come out of General Motors on Retirement and Social Security.

The new Psychiatrist that was counseling me after several sessions with him; that it is not worth going through what you have to go through with General Motors if I wanted to come out he would take me out he did not know the procedure in during so; but he would support me one hundred percent. My prayers were answered and I was led to file another Civil Rights lawsuit through an African American lawyer by the name of Fred Greene, who was thirty five years old at the time. And since my Psychiatrist Doctor took me off work on disability. I had to go through a Workers Compensation trial and the Lord Jesus blessed me with a sixty thousand dollars settlement and the remaining two thousand from the first lawsuit was dismissed and I could continue my second lawsuit in Circuit Court in Charlotte, Michigan. It was a town very hostile toward blacks and known for its Ku Klux Klan activities.

I also received Total and Permanent Disability Retirement and I also received Social Security; and all three of our children received Social Security checks each month. And I gave all of their money to them. In the second Civil Rights Lawsuit in Charlotte, Michigan

Judge Thomas Eveland said I did not have a Civil Rights case and I ended up having to pay General Motors attorney fees of Fifty-Eight thousand dollars. The Judge said it was a contract violation; for the suggestions; which was not tried in the first Lawsuit; although General Motors attorney tried to prove it was taking up in the first Lawsuit; but they did not prevail. My attorney was so outdone with this Lawsuit; that he said the jury only came back with twenty thousand dollars. We did not even get twenty-five thousand dollars so we will have to appeal the case.

In the summer of June two thousand, my attorney Fred Greene called me from Mississippi; where he had taking a teaching position at some University Teaching Law, and his brother Anthony Green who was an attorney from Grand Rapids assisted him; told me it is time to give it up; it's been going on for seventeen years and General Motors is not going to give you anything? I said No! The Lord Jesus did not bring me this far to quit. A few days later he called me and said that General Motors told their attorney to ask him; to ask me; how much would I take to settle the lawsuit? I told him how much I would take to settle the case. He called me a few days later and said he had good news for me; that General Motors is going to give you what you asked for to settle the case.

In 2008 Dr. William T. BeeCroft my Psychiatrist sent me to see a Neuropsychologist in Haslett, Michigan to be evaluated for Alzheimer's Dementia. I had been seeing Dr. BeeCroft for eighteen years. He sent me to my appointment to see Dr. Dennis M. Pelon on June 23, 2008; because he detected that I could be suffering from Alzheimer's. After turning in my paperwork to his wife and after taking the test he had me to sit in the lobby and my wife had arrived for the test results; after being called into his office he told my wife and I that I have Alzheimer's and in seven years I would be bedridden; but by taking the medication it would slow it down a couple of years. And he wanted me to continue to see Dr. Hilton Thomas my Psychologist who is African American, who I have been seeing since May 15, 1985.

And I had been under a couple other Psychiatrist prior to Dr. BeeCroft taking over their practice. On January 20, 2011 was my second appointment to be tested to see how far the Alzheimer's had advance and to what stage. After my wife asked Dr. Dennis M. Pelon some questions prior to being tested or evaluated for Alzheimer's. He acted like he got stirred and said he has Alzheimer's and he have been in practice for thirty years and he goes by whatever the test results are. After the diagnosis or evaluation, he told us that my condition was steadily deteriorating and he wanted me to have a professional driver to ride with me to see if I am capable of driving alone. And he wanted to see me again in one to two years to see if I am capable of driving alone; and, to see how much my condition had deteriorated to see if I needed Supervision.

On April 12, 2011. I told Dr. William T. BeeCroft my Psychiatrist at my last appointment after eighteen years; that I was in our Church Convention in Louisville, Kentucky; when the music and choir started a song and all the Ministry stood up and then the people in the congregation followed. Every time I would look up at the words of the song on the screen the Holy Spirit would bring tears to my eyes and I would start crying in the Spirit with joy unspeakable and full of glory. And I had to turn my eyes away from the screen to keep from crying out loud; because I did not want to bring attention to myself. The tears was tears of joy from Jesus the son of God Holy Spirit and it felt so heavenly and it was so great and fulfilling. The next day which was Sunday we had Church Service from ten O'clock in the morning till one O'clock in the afternoon. Then we had prayer for the Saints and blessed the delicious nutritional food; before departing on our way back home to many parts of the States and other countries.

After dinner and leaving the Church; as soon as I took the exit to the expressway the Holy Spirit came upon me and I automatically started crying real hard and the Holy Spirit was actually, literally moving my upper body for about two to three minutes; then it would leave again for two to three minutes with joy unspeakable and full of glory as it said in 1 PETER 1: 8 Whom having not seen, ye love; in whom, though now ye see him not, yet believing, ye rejoice with joy unspeakable and full of glory. I thought about the scripture in PSALMS 126:5 they that sow in tears shall reap in joy. This went on for about three hours off and on. And it was revealed to me the

God of Heaven and Earth through His beloved son had healed me of Alzheimer's and every disease or illness; that were associated with the two Civil Rights lawsuits. I knew this was the confirmation that I had been healed completely. And I have not been the same since that miraculous manifestation of the Holy Spirit.

He told me lots of his clients have said the same thing; but they always come back. I told him I know for a fact that I want be back. He told me in three months that I would be dead if I did not see him; and he was not coming to my funeral. My wife also was there at the appointment (Cathie Cobb Hudson) I told him No! He said you are going to die? I said not if Jesus Christ comes back for his 'Bride' the Church or theirs a restore Church once again on the earth like it was in the early Church in the time of 'Jesus' Five Gifted Anointed Ministry on the earth in the latter days; that raised the dead, the blinded eyes were open, the lame were walking, the deaf and dumb were hearing and speaking and evil spirits were cast out of those that were possessed of demons. In HAGGI 2: 9 the glory of this latter house shall be greater than of the former, saith the Lord of hosts: and in this place will I give peace, saith the Lord of hosts. The latter rain is still to come and it's going to rain down Spiritual Gifts from third Heaven where God and Jesus and the Angelic Host resides, and the Tabernacle in the wilderness in the old Testament and the Temple in the New Testament are a type of the same setup in Third Heaven.

He practically begged me to take the medication. I answered No! I know how the Holy Spirit the life of God came upon me, and I received a complete healing. He said at least let him make me a six month appointment for me. I said I will come for one reason to glorify the God of Heaven and Earth; for His beloved son Jesus Christ for a testimony. Then on April 14, 2011. I had my last appointment with Dr. Hilton Thomas, PHD. A license Psychologist and Baptist Minister and now the Pastor of his church. I gave him the same explanation that I gave to Dr. BeeCroft. How God through His beloved son Jesus Christ had miraculously healed me from Alzheimer's and every disease or illness that was associated with the lawsuits the Lord Jesus have blessed me to be victorious. He told me in front of my wife that in three months I would be calling him.

I told him No! This will be my last visit; since May 15, 1985. He laughed and said I know you want, your wife will; because you won't be able. When we were at the entrance to leave I looked back at him and he was waving at my wife; but avoiding me.

I went to my six month appointment with Dr. William T. BeeCroft M.D. Board CERTIFICATE PSYCHIATRY at Ingham Regional Medical Center. When he came into the waiting room to get me; for the session; in his office he said he wanted to take my blood pressure; which he knew it would not fit over my wrist. He was nervous and he asked me if I needed any medication. I said I did not take any medication; since I was completely healed by the Holy Spirit. He asked me, how do you feel? I answered I feel great! He told me he did not know what he could do for me; but if I ever needed his help the door will always be open for me.

On May 9, 2012 at my next appointment with Dr. Dennis Pelon, Ph. D: P.C. Neuropsychology and rehabilitation Services in Haslett, Michigan. I also had the opportunity to witness to his wife before he came into the front office or waiting room to get me for the evaluation testing. During the testing he kept saying very good, very good, very good, I knew many of the answers before he had everything set-up. After about three hours of testing. This is what he wrote down, after I had given him my testimony of how the God of Heaven and earth had miraculously healed me of the incurable disease of Alzheimer's through His beloved son Jesus Christ.

(SUMMARY) He told me he had compare the test scores of JUNE 23, 2008. He told me he had compare the test scores of June 23, 2008. And the scores at present shows you no longer have Alzheimer's; because if you still had Alzheimer's your condition would have gotten progressively worst in four years; but mine have gotten progressively better. This lets him know I no longer have Alzheimer's. He also wrote down: The male who experienced a Spiritual awakening approximately six months ago was reevaluated after a sixteen month interval. His condition has clearly improved, he is very optimistic and jubilant in his presentation, and minimizes any concerns regarding any cognitive limitations at present. Current testing reveal significant improvement in complex attention and visual-spatial. Memory functions, the patient is without evidence of clinical depression, hypomania, pain, hallucinations delusions, or homicidal ideation. Praise God! He also wanted to see me again in one to two years for reevaluation purposes.

On June 26, 2014 my last appointment with Dr. Dennis Pelon Ph.D.: PC Neuropsychology (Alzheimer's Doctor). My wife came to the appointment office; after the testing in the waiting area, when he came in to get us to go over the results; he said your memory is still intact; it has not changed. In MATTHEW 18:16 but if he will not hear thee, then take with thee one or two more, that in the mouth of two or three witnesses let every word be established. I had four Neuropsychology (Alzheimer's) appointments to confirm that I was miraculously healed by the Holy Spirit. I had one prescription filled in 2008 and I did not finish the month supply; because I believed that I had worked so hard as a Born Again Christian in the Non-Denominational Pentecostal Faith and the same faith with works by the Holy Spirit took me through two Civil rights lawsuits would heal me of Alzheimer's.

In ST. LUKE 4:25 but I tell you of a truth, many widows were in Israel in the days of Elias, when the heaven was shut up for three years and six months, when a great famine was throughout the land; (26) But unto none of them was Elias sent, save unto SAREPTA, a city of Sidon unto a woman that was a widow. 27 And many lepers were in Israel in the time of Eliseus the prophet; and none of them was cleanse, saving Naaman the Syrian. In the news Media it said; today, there are no survivors of Alzheimer's disease. Worldwide, there are at least 47,000,000 people living with Alzheimer's and other dementias; in the United States alone someone develops Alzheimer's every 67 seconds and without change, could grow to every 33 seconds by 2050. Worldwide there are 47,000,000, are living with dementia.

I am the only Born Again Christian in The Non-Denominational Pentecostal Faith, and Pentecostal Faith; that was diagnosed with the incurable disease of Alzheimer's on 6/23/2008 and was told in seven years I would be bedridden. And again on 1/20/2011 after the testing the doctor said your condition is steadily deteriorating and he did not want me driving a vehicle until I had been evaluated by a professional driving instructor; and he wanted to see me again in one to two years. I saw him for the third time on 5/9/2012 and after the testing he said theirs is no sign of Alzheimer's. I had giving him my testimony of how the Holy Spirit had taking complete control of my life on the expressway for about three hours off and on and I know I was completely healed of every disease that occurred in the First lawsuit and continual on from August 19, 1983 until present August 1, 2015. He said it could come back so he gave me another appointment on 6/26/2014 and after the testing he said your memory is still intact and he sent me to a specialist for a cat scan and everything was fine and he still made another appointment for me to see him in a year and it will be on August 18, 2015.

It will be Fifty-Three days since I was diagnosed to be bedridden with the mind boggling disease of Alzheimer's and my next appointment on 8/18/2015 I was diagnosed to be bedridden in seven years; which would have been on 6/23/2015. I was miraculously healed by the power invested in me by the power of the Holy Spirit and I have never asked anybody to pray for me. I have always prayed for myself; because I am the only person that knows the life I have lived for 'Jesus Christ' and the results has been great; ever since the Holy Spirit healed me; when I hear a Spiritual song with a beautiful anointed melody; the tears began to flow and my hands and body began to move just like on the day of Pentecost, which has continue to live in those who are called chosen and faithful. I can be at Church or at home or in my car and when I am touched by the Holy Spirit the tears began to flow down my cheek and sometime at church I have to hold the tears back to keep from crying aloud and could disturb the service or keep someone else from getting there blessing by being distracted by me.

And it is the same Holy Spirit that took complete control of my life; for about three hours on and off; on the expressway in Louisville, Kentucky is still present in my life and it's glorious to behold. Another example is in 2 KINGS 20:1-11 in those days was Hezekiah sick unto death. And the Prophet Isaiah the son of Amoz came to him, and said unto him, thus saith the Lord, set thine house in order; for thou shalt die, and not live (2) then he turned his face to the wall, and prayed unto the Lord, saying (3) I beseech thee, O Lord, remember now how I have walked before thee in truth and with a perfect heart, and have done that which is good in thy sight. And Hezekiah wept sore. (4) And it came to pass, afore Isaiah was gone out into the middle court that the word of the Lord came to him, saying (5) Turn again, and tell Hezekiah the captain of my people, thus saith the Lord, the God of David thy Father, "I have heard thy prayer, I have seen thy tears: behold, I will heal thee: on the third day thou shalt go up unto the house of the Lord.

(6) And I will add unto thy days fifteen years; and I will deliver thee and this city out of the hand of the king of Assyrian and I will defend this city for mine own sake, and for my servant David's sake. (7) Isaiah said, take a lump of figs, and they took and laid it on the boil, and he recovered. (8) And Hezekiah said unto Isaiah, "What shall be the sign that the Lord will heal me, and that I shall go up into the house of the Lord the third day? (9) And Isaiah said, this sign shalt thou have of the Lord, that the Lord will do the thing that he hath spoken, shall the shadow go forward ten degrees, or go back ten degrees? (10) And Hezekiah answered, it is a light thing for the shadow to go down ten degrees. (11) And Isaiah the prophet cried unto the Lord: and he brought the shadow ten degrees backward, by which it had gone down in the dial Ahaz.

This miracle of God giving Isaiah the Prophet words to King Hezekiah for his healing was similar to God healing me of Alzheimer's and the Holy Spirit began the healing process at our Church Convention Center. And then it took complete control of my life after leaving for home alone to Lansing, Michigan from Louisville, Kentucky. I knew I was completely healed of all the illnesses or sicknesses of all I had been going through with the two lawsuits back to back against General Motors for seventeen years from August 19, 1983 to July 27, 2000 and the continuation until 6/26/2014. On my second healing confirmation. And it has been ordained and substantiated that my motive for standing up for Jesus Christ and his righteousness extended my life.

The Apostle Paul in his letter he wrote to the Church in Romans 15: 4 for whatsoever things were written aforetime were written for our learning, that we through patience and comfort of the scriptures might have hope. Also Apostle Paul wrote a letter to the church in 1 CORINTHIANS 10:11 now all these things happened unto them for ensamples, and they are written for our admonition, upon whom the ends of the world are come. These two scriptures explains why the bible was written and its purpose for our lives.

    I also had high blood pressure for twenty six years and it was devastating in my life and trying to work at General Motors and getting so dizzy and light headed that I had to sit down and drink some cold water or go to the rest room and lay on the cold floor till I fell strong enough to wash my face with cold water, and all the times I had to go to first aid to get my blood pressure checked and lay down till I felt well enough to go back to work. And doing housework or cutting the grass I had to stop several times for feeling dizzy and faint hearted, and all the times I had to go to the bathroom at home to lay on the cold floor, then wash my face with cold water. I have fallen on the bathroom floor and my wife heard the noise and rushed to help me; but all that went away when I was healed completely of all my illnesses and sicknesses; when the Holy Spirit came upon me with a great love coming home from our Church Convention on the expressway from Louisville, Kentucky.

    I had another miracle that happened again on my way home from our Church Convention in Indianapolis, Indiana during the Labor Day weekend in 2013. I was listening to my Mother old cassette tape recorder enjoying the teaching from possibly the seventies and I was going at least seventy miles an hour when all of a sudden I notice the car ahead of me was not moving. I slammed on my brakes about three to four car lengths ahead of me and my car tires was spinning just as fast in the back of the car ahead of me. And I should have been covering up; but I was so calm and when I should have impacted I sensed the Holy Spirit come between my car, and the car in front of me moved up slowly and stop and move up a little more then I notice my car was spinning in place and when the car in from of me had moved up a car length my car slid right in that exact space and stopped.

I rolled down my window and looked outside to see what the problem was and there was cars lined up as far as I could see and I say it was at least forty cars ahead of me, I used that number because the number forty is a biblical number. The early Church operated in a perfect working order with all the God Gifted Apostles; only lasted forty years, and the Prophet Moses had three periods of Forty Years in his life and he died at one hundred and twenty years old so there must have been an accident or a vehicle stopped on the expressway or a highway crew working on some project. Therefore every car had to move right at the precise time in order for my car not to slam into the car in front of me, and there were a couple of people in the back seat of the car ahead of me, and they could have been children in the back seat; and as fast as I was going on the expressway; there could have been a chain reaction and I would have been killed or seriously injured and the people in front of me. And my car would have be demolished.

I noticed just prior to their car moving up I sensed the Holy Spirit came between our cars. I knew it was the Spirit of God manifested through His beloved son Jesus Christ. The Holy Spirit is the life of God. Just like there is only one sun in the whole universe; but the rays of the sun can be felt all over the world; so it is also with God's Holy Spirit.

There is only one God; but His Spirit permeates the whole universe. The Holy Spirit took complete control of my car and cause all those cars to move up at the appointed time. Jesus the son of God intervene in my behalf; because of the price I have paid in applying the pure unadulterated word of God to my life; for being taught, Holiness, Righteousness, Perfection is not an option; but is necessary and vital to strive to be like Jesus Christ, God's only begotten son. And no telling all the hundreds of times I have testify; that I am doing everything possible to become like Christ, that's how I have been taught and instructed in the word of God. I have quoted 1Peter 2:21-25 (there's been hundreds of times through my forty-two years as a Born Again Christian in the Non-Denominational Pentecostal Church. Our ministers will not in any form or fashion compromise the word of God. I have been taught if we love truth we will stay;

if God had brought you here; if not; you will not stay and blend in with the masses in religion) 21 For even hereunto were ye called; because Christ also suffered for us, leaving us an example, that ye should follow his steps. 22 Who did no sin, neither was guile found in his mouth. 23 Who when he was reviled, reviled not again; when he suffered, he threatened not; but committed himself to him that judgeth righteously. 24 Who his own self bare our sins in his own body on the tree, that we, being dead to sins, should live unto righteousness, by whose stripes ye were healed. 25 For ye were as sheep going astray; but are now returned unto the shepherd and Bishop of your souls.

I have done everything humanly possible to become like my Lord and Saviour Jesus Christ the only begotten of the Father in truth and righteousness, and I have been awarded accordingly. I have been hospitalized for being suicidal and having my stomach pumped for overdosing on prescription pills. My Psychologist Dr. Hilton T. Thomas have called the hospital to admit me after having my stomach pumped; then an ambulance would take me to a mental Hospital. Twice I was at Pine Rest Christian Hospital in Grand Rapids, Michigan, Twice at St. Lawrence Hospital in Lansing, Michigan. Once at Ingham medical Hospital, Once at the Mental Hospital in Jackson, Michigan, and once in the Mental Hospital in Owosso, Michigan. That is seven times. And there could have been a couple more times.

All the many times my wife and three children came to visit me, my medical doctor at Mid-Michigan Physicians diagnose me with high prostate levels. I heard him tell his assistance; how come you did not catch the high prostate level the last time he was here? And he said to him everything was normal at that time; so Dr. Abdullah, M.D. sent me to the Health Clinic at Michigan State University to see the Urologist, Dr. Davis in the summer of 2013. I first gave him my testimony of Jesus healing me of Alzheimer's and it was confirmed with medical evidence; and I gave him a New Citizen Press Newspaper, when I was honor as Lansing First 'BLACK' "Boxer of the Year' for 'BLACK' History Month of February, with an article about my first book, 'Boxer of the Year' Hudson VGM. I also have a live free website. I was also told him that prostate runs in our family. My Father died from Prostate Cancer and my oldest brother has it and I have an uncle and one of his sons have prostate. After the testing he went to check the results; when he returned with the results; he said you have nothing to worry about.

I was under my medical doctor for twenty-six years being treated for High Blood Pressure. I was under a Psychologist for twenty-six years; and a Psychiatrist for 21 years and I was admitted to at least seven Mental Hospitals. I was miraculously healed of all of my illnesses by God's mighty Holy Spirit power manifested through His beloved son Jesus Christ 'JESUS CHRIST' and it was confirmed with 'MEDICAL EVIDENCE' ON MAY 9, 2012 and on June 26, 2014.

If in this life I do His will, I will see His plan through shrouded be, I will understand His out reached hand, that pleads, come follow me. If in his steps I follow close I will rest in cherished dreams, at end of my life, I will rise to meet, the king on clouds of wings. To His abode with joy I will sing of his amazing grace. It took His blood and my resolve to make it to this place. On his dear word soul did feed, where his true saints were fed, and to this place I walk by faith, and thus was Spirit led. Turn back a voice would often cry, you're destined to the pit; but from the bible page I found. The light my pathway lit. Oh, come along all blood bought ones, into the shelter high, on wings of faith forward go, you are destined for the sky. AMEN!!!

First Survival of Alzheimer's

LANSING COMMUNITY COLLEGE
"Commencement"
June 14, 1981

Draft Strips Three Champs of Titl[e]
Uncle Sam Delivers

RUDY GUERRERO

ELMO HUDSON

Uncle Sam delivered a few body blows to the Lansing District Golden Gloves Tournament this year. The draft, which has been stepped up due to the war in Vietnam, has eliminated several of last year's top performers.

Three champions and three of last year's finalists will be missing this year due to the draft.

The tournament's two greatest losses will be state champion Rudy Guerrero and state finalist Elmo Hudson. Both were favorites in last year's tournament. Guerrero, who won the open flyweight title by default in 1964, and missed the 1965 tournament, battled his way to the state bantamweight crown in the service division last year. He decisioned Portland's Robert Wheeler to [win] the district crown, then decisioned Al Benavides of Saginaw to claim the state championship.

Hudson, fighting for Saginaw Opportunity Center, won the district open featherweight title, topping David Ford, Owosso, and was defeated [by] Boston Robertson of Grand Rapids in the state finals.

KO Blow to Glovers

Another district champ who has entered the armed forces is Tony Kelly of Dimondale who won the sub-novice middleweight title. Kelly earned a pair of decisions and won the title with a '36 technical knockout over Ron Rodgers of Owosso.

Finalists lost to the armed forces are Don Marlett of Dimondale, Vic Trierweiler of Portland and Carlos Valle of St. Johns. Trierweiler lost in the finals to Tony Robledo of Owosso in the lightheavyweight open division.

Marlett dropped a close decision to teammate Jim Warren in the finals of the novice middleweight division, and Valle was edged by Wayne Woods for the novice featherweight crown.

"We've lost some good boys to the draft," said Al VanNess, head Lansing trainer and matchmaker for the tournament. "It will hurt our open class more than any other."

All of the major teams, co-champions Portland and Dimondale, Caravan, Russell's Cleaners, which is replacing last year's SOC entry, and St. Johns will be affected by the loss, with Dimondale being hurt the most. Marlett and Kelly combined to earn seven team points for Dimondale last year.

First Survival of Alzheimer's

Elmo Hudson

ELMO HUDSON

BOXER OF THE YEAR — Elmo Hudson, three-time district Golden Gloves champion, was named winner of the Boxer of the Year trophy by Francis Shepard at the annual Golden Gloves dinner Wednesday. Shepard, former boxer and now a referee, said Hudson's victory over two state champions in the district tournament earned him the trophy. Hudson lost in the state finals last weekend, but it was later discovered he was boxing with three broken ribs. All Lansing tournament Golden Glovers were honored by the Capital Caravan Shriners Club.

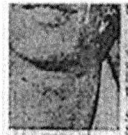

Jim Wallington
Stemler Seeks Rematch With Lansing's Hudson

Doug Stemler wants another boxing match with Elmo Hudson.

After the Portland boxer raised Hudson's hand in victory after their Golden Glove match last week, Stemler was trying to arrange a rematch. It could come in a amateur club show this winter or spring.

Hudson, defending his open featherweight (126 pounds) title, handed Stemler his first defeat in the semi-finals of the Lansing district tournament. Fans are still talking about the fight, heralded as one of the best in recent years.

Both boxers admitted conditioning was the key to Hudson's triumph.

"I wasn't even out of breath at the end of the fight," said Hudson who represents Service Opportunity Center in the tournament. "I trained hard, knowing I would have to fight Stemler and knowing I probably would have to go three rounds to win. Most of my training is based on building my wind."

Stemler, still trying to catch his breath in the dressing room, said:

"I've never seen a boxer in better condition. He was still moving just as fast in the third round as he was in the first minute of the fight. I thought I was in condition, but compared to Elmo, I wasn't. After the first round I was drooping and swinging wild. Man, is he ever quick.

"And who said he couldn't hit hard? He hurt me more than other boxers. He's just about the best I've faced."

Stemler then turned to Portland trainer Bob Hirschman and said, "If you get me another bout with Hudson, I'll train faithfully and hard up to the fight, no matter when it is."

"Elmo was the better fighter tonight," Stemler mumbled. "I was proud to hold his hand up in victory. But next time..."

And as he walked out of the room, you had the feeling that Stemler wished he was Darel Ford this week. Ford is the

Hudson   Stemler

Owosso boy who faces Hudson this week in the finals. Ford, like Stemler, won a state novice title last year. And that impresses Hudson who'll work as hard this week to win the title.

Hudson didn't underestimate Stemler. For the entire week before the match he and trainer Herschel Roper concentrated on beating the Portland High School student from Sunfield.

"We knew Stemler had a dangerous punch," said Roper, a former Golden Gloves champion. "He had seven knockouts in his eight victories. We had to stop his right hand. And that's what we did. After Stemler would throw his right, Hudson would block it and then move inside quickly with a 1-2 combination and sometimes a third punch. Elmo simply wore him out with his punches and tremendous conditioning."

Dave Shaw, another former Gloves champion now training the Caravan Center team, marveled at Hudson's victory.

"The most remarkable thing was the way Elmo brought up his hands in defense and held them high during the three rounds With his hands high, he had great protection against Stemler's haymaker and kept his hands in better position to counter.

"Elmo used to hold his left hand down like most young boxers. But I never saw a kid hold his hands in the right position for three rounds.

"And don't worry, Elmo will be ready for this week. He doesn't get overconfident and he wants to win the state championship."

There's still plenty of room in the Civic Center for this Wednesday's Lansing district finals, but the same story isn't true for the state finals in Grand Rapids this Saturday.

If any Lansing or area fan wants to attend the one-night show in Grand Rapids, he should phone the Civic Auditorium early this week. They will reserve seats for you if you follow up with a money order. Lansing's support has been sparse in recent years and officials here would like to see a large local delegation at the state finals.

FIRST SURVIVAL OF ALZHEIMER'S

Stemlar, Hudson, Ford Seek Gloves Crown
3 Champs Eye Same

 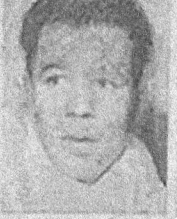 

ELMO HUDSON — Lansing SOC
DOUG STEMLAR — Portland
DAREL FORD — Owosso

Three 1965 Gloves Winners Seek Same Open Featherweight Crown

Venturi Back on Top After 'Lucky' Win

February 12, 2012 - February 25, 2012

Lansing's First African American to win "Boxer of the Year", Elmo Hudson Pen's Book

"The Hudson-Stemlar match was by far the best in what was termed the most outstanding boxing show..." - Jim Wallington, State Journal Sportswriter, 1966

Purchase your copy today by calling 888.280.7715. Log on to authorhouse.com, amazon.com or barnesandnoble.com to order online.

First Survival of Alzheimer's

Elmo	Hudson
Author/Elmo Hudson	Male
▮▮▮▮	A517-230-4242
Boxer of the Year	Hudson v Gtu
▮▮▮▮	Lansing
Eaton	Detroit
Eastern	5173210349
▮▮▮▮	
elmohudson@yahoo.com	S-C 17.50-H-C 28.95
None	
1-4107-1940-5 (e-book)	
1-4107-1941-3 (Paperback)	
1-4107-1942-1 (Hardcover)	10/14/03
233617/14591	236 pgs
Anytime	
Lmo	
Mr. or Brother Elmo	

Gospel Assembly non-denominational Pentecostal Church, Prison Ministry, Ex offender release reentry program, USA Fitness Spa, witnessing door to door, on Television etc.,
Retired-General Motors
Yes-Everything
Non-Apply
William T BeeCroft, M.D, Board Certified Psychiatry Ingham Regional Medical Center, 517.975.3200, Fax 517.995-3216. 2727 S. Pennsylvania Avenue Lansing, Michigan 48910. www.irmc.org.
Dr. Hilton T Thomas Professional Psychological & Rehabilitation Services P.C. 302 S Waverly Road, Suite1, Lansing, Michigan 48917 (517-321-5900)-Fax (517-321-5945).
Dennis M. Pelon, PHD,P.C.Neuropsychology and Rehabilitation Services 1640 Haslett Rd. Suite 110, Haslett, MI 48840. 517-339-1686, Fax. 517-339-3286.
Ashraf ABullah, MD. International Medicine Mid-Michigan Physicians (517-913-3810), e-mail www.mmponline.com. Fax (517-9133811) 1540 Lake Lansing Rd
Lansing, Michigan 48912.
Michigan Department of Civil Rights, State of Michigan Plaza Building, 1200 Sixth Avenue, Detroit, Michigan 48226.
GMC-BOC Plant #1, 920 townsend street Lansing, MI 48933
William R. Schultz (p-29147) Foster, Swift, Collins &Smith, 313 south Washington Square, Lansing, Michigan 48933 (517-372-8050).
Mr. Arthur Sheffey, Department of Civil Rights 333 South Capital Town center BLDG-2nd floor, Lansing, Michigan 48913 (517-323-3591, May 16, 1989.
GM Pension Administration Center, P.O. Box 5014, Southfield MI 48086-5014, 1800-489-4646.

Lansing Business University -1 Year
Lansing Community College- Associate Degree- Religion or Philosophy.

PATIENT'S AUTHORIZATION FOR RELEASE OF HEALTH RECORDS
REQUEST TO RELEASE OR OBTAIN RECORDS

This form for Authorization for Release of Protected Health Information is designed to comply with Title 42 of Federal Regulations, Part 2 (regarding alcohol and substance abuse records) and/or state laws respecting confidentiality of records and patient communications with mental health professionals, other healthcare providers and medical center support staff.

Patient's Name: Hudson, Elmo, NMN

Address: [redacted]

Social Security Number: [redacted]   Date of Birth: 10/8/43

The undersigned hereby authorizes and requests Provider:

McLaren Multi-Specialty Clinic — Dr. Beecroft
2727 S. Pennsylvania Ave.
Lansing, MI 48910

to release any and all information contained in the records of patient listed above, INCLUDING INFORMATION REGARDING DRUG AND/OR ALCOHOL TREATMENT, PSYCHOLOGICAL, AND SOCIAL SERVICES RECORDS, COMMUNICATIONS MADE TO A SOCIAL WORKER, PSYCHOLOGIST OR PSYCHIATRIST, AND HIV/AIDS/AIDS-RELATED COMPLEX DOCUMENTATION, to the individual(s) or organizations listed below, by providing copies of medical/hospital records to:

Elmo Hudson
[redacted]

Include dates of treatment for requested information: 18 years

Indicate any limitations to disclosure: None

PURPOSE FOR SUCH DISCLOSURE – AT THE REQUEST OF:
☐ Provider for Continued Care ☐ Attorney ☒ Patient ☐ Court ☐ Insurance ☐ Other

I understand that unless I revoke this authorization, it will expire in 60 days from the date signed. I understand that I may revoke this Authorization at any time, except to the extent that action has been taken in reliance upon it. I may revoke this authorization by contacting, in writing, the Provider that maintains the identified protected health information. I understand that I may refuse to sign this authorization and that the Provider will not condition treatment or payment on my providing this authorization (except to the extent that the authorization is for research-related treatment, in which case the Provider may refuse to provide that research-related treatment). I understand that Michigan law allows the Provider to charge a reasonable fee for the requested copies of the medical record.

Signature: Elmo Hudson   Date: April 1, 2013

If signed by a legal representative, indicate his/her relationship to patient (parent, guardian, conservator, etc.) and attach legal documentation:

Witness: Janiya Decater   Date: April 1, 2013

THIS FORM MUST BE FILED IN THE PATIENT'S MEDICAL RECORD
(Authorization to Release or Obtain Information)

MAY 09 2013
MAY 09 2013

Outpatient Psychotherapy Progress Note

Date: March 27, 2008   Time Start: 10:45 AM   Time End: 11:10 AM

Patient Name: Elmo Hudson   Birthdate: 10-8-43

Allergies: NKMA

PCP: Dr. Abdullah

Current medications:

Prozac 60mg p.o. qhs daily
Abilify 30mg p.o. qd

Other medications:
Prinvil 40mg p.o. qd; Zocor 20mg p.o. qam

Current clinical status and Mental Status Examination:
This is a well-developed well-nourished African-American male seen for evaluation and treatment of his depression. Mood is generally euthymic; affect is broad. Speech is without production abnormality. Thought content reveals suicidal thoughts but no plan, this was identified by Dr Thomas who sent me a email, Pt states these have started after he developed auditory hallucinations(again he has not revealed this to me on prior visit) patient does express continued delusional thinking but less so than previously. Cognitive function: he is oriented to person, place, time, day, date, year, and reason for the evaluation. Judgment is poor; insight is poor; remote, intermediate, and short-term memory are intact. He denies absence episodes dissociations or any frank seizure activity denies any plan to harm self or anyone else

Response and Side Effects of Medication:
patient denies significant side effects of is medication protocol he still continues to have a residual amount of psychotic thinking (paranoid). he has continued modest depressive sx due to the financial stress he is under chronically, he now reveals suicidal thoughts due to auditory hallucinations which are new for him. and has had some recurrence of paranoid thinking that he was a victim of a "scam". He has continued to have severe financial stresses.

Labs Reviewed:
Patient was informed of the Black box warning with the use of Abilify the need for a comprehensive profile, lipid profile and glycolatedhemaglobin. The patient does resist getting these laboratory examinations done when given a lab test paperwork. He continues to not want lab tests done.

Content of Session:
primarily reality testing. We reviewed exercise and behavioral interventions. Reviewed exercise and its benefit- generally has reasons not to exercise even though his chole high

Therapeutic Intervention/Progress Towards Treatment Goals:

Hudson, Elmo
8/18/15
Page 2

Memory and new learning capabilities tested largely intact with subtle suppression in encoding only for one subtest. His recall of conversational details was at only the 5th percentile during immediate acquisition (10/24), but at 30 minutes delay recall obtained the 50th percentile with 9/12 units of conversational detail accurately recalled at 30 minutes delay. There was a 90% retention rate versus 75% observed previously on a comparable measure. Verbal learning process through repetition and cueing was intact with acquisition across 4 learning trials at the 37th percentile and recall at 30 minutes delay at the 63rd percentile with 6/10 words accurately recalled spontaneously at 30 minutes delay. This compares with previous performance on a similar measure at the 73rd percentile level. Recognition memory format revealed intact recognition or storage of the newly acquired information with a score of 20/20 obtained.

Executive function assessment revealed continuing functional impairment involving the ability to sequentially reason, plan, and monitor performance according to rules and procedures. Planning and sequential reasoning remain at the 3rd percentile on the Tower of London Test with speed of problem solving at the 59th percentile and self-monitoring capacity at the 9th percentile level. There were 2 rule-following errors consistent with previous test results. He had difficulty keeping in mind the rules and procedures and monitoring behavior accordingly while performing tasks requiring reasoning or planning. His ability to generate alternative ideas and plans was at the 50th percentile on the Controlled Oral Word Association Test versus 70th percentile obtained previously. He had one rule-following error and loss of mental set error observed reflecting the difficulty with self-monitoring as noted above. Category Fluency Test results further revealed normal range access to semantic memory network obtaining the 63rd percentile versus 84th percentile previously. He demonstrated some mild difficulty with inhibiting previous modes of responding and shifting mental set with 2 errors observed on the Luria Go-No-Go Test consistent with previous test results.

Speech and language functions showed signs of decline in capacity to name common objects from memory with the patient able to accurately name only 26/60 objects falling below the 1st percentile versus a previous result of 40/60 obtained. His ability to decipher meaning from sentence structure and execute sequential verbal commands was below normal as before with Token Test results at 36/44 obtaining the 2nd percentile.

Sensory perceptual examination was negative for a lateralized pattern of tactile, auditory, or visual imperception under conditions of double simultaneous stimulation. Visual-spatial perception of direction was normal range on the Line Orientation subtest with a score of 15/20 obtaining the 38th percentile level. Visual integration and object recognition were, however, below normal as before with Hopkins Verbal Learning Test results at 15/30 falling below the 1st percentile. Previous results were at 16/30. There were 8 isolate responses reflecting difficulty to misperceive parts as whole objects and inability to integrate visual details and some impulsivity in his visual perceptual capacity.

Motor function assessment revealed a drop in grip strength bilaterally with 28.5 kgms of strength obtaining only the 2nd percentile versus 39.7 kgms of strength observed previously on the right. Left-sided grip strength was at 25.7 kgms or 2nd percentile versus 33 kgms observed previously. Visual integration and assembly were normal range at the 37th percentile on the Figure Copy subtest. As noted above, visual-spatial memory was also intact at 30 minutes delay with reproduction of the same figure from memory.

Geriatric Depression Scale results (0) failed to reveal evidence of clinically significant depression at time of testing. Pain level was at 8/10 in his right shoulder owing to a recent injury. There were no hallucinations, delusions or suicidal ideation, there was no pressured speech or flight of ideas, and he has only minimal preoccupation at present with the family conflict noted in history.

www.ingramcontent.com/pod-product-compliance
Ingram Content Group UK Ltd.
Pitfield, Milton Keynes, MK11 3LW, UK
UKHW022225230426
12048UKWH00016BA/1066